THE LANGUAGE OF IMAGES IN ROMAN A

This book develops a new theory for the understanding of Roman pictorial art. By treating Roman art as a semantic system it establishes a connection between artistic forms and the ideological messages contained within. The history of Roman art traditionally followed the model of a sequence of stylistic phases affecting the works of their era in the manner of a uniform *Zeitgeist*. In contrast, the author shows different stylistic forms being used for different themes and messages. This leads to the reception of Greek models, a basic phenomenon of Roman art, appearing in a new light. The formulations of specific messages are established from Greek art types of different eras: Classical forms for the grandeur of the state, for example. Different stylistic forms from the Greek past serve to express Roman ideological values. In this way a conceptual and comprehensible pictorial language arose, uniting the multicultural population of the Roman state.

TONIO HÖLSCHER is Professor of Classical Archaeology at the University of Heidelberg. His publications focus on public monuments, political iconography and urbanism in Ancient Greece and Rome and on general art and cultural theory. He is a member of various scientific institutions, including the Academia Europae, London.

ANTHONY SNODGRASS was Laurence Professor of Classical Archaeology at Cambridge from 1976 to 2001, before which he had taught at the University of Edinburgh. His teaching career of forty years covered nearly every aspect of Greek and Roman archaeology, though he came to specialise in pre-Classical Greece. His publications include *The Dark Age of Greece* (1971), *Archaic Greece* (1980), *An Archaeology of Greece* (1987) and *Homer and the Artists* (1998).

ANNEMARIE KÜNZL-SNODGRASS is Language Teaching Officer in the Department of German at the University of Cambridge and Lektorin at Jesus College, Cambridge, specialising in the teaching of 'ab initio' German and the development of teaching materials for computer-assisted language learning. She is co-author of a revision guide to German grammar, *Upgrade your German* (2003), and the interactive CD-ROM *Video Plus German* (2003).

JAŚ ELSNER is Humfry Payne Senior Research Fellow in Classical Art and Archaeology at Corpus Christi College, Oxford, and author of various studies in Roman art history including *Art and the Roman Viewer* (1995) and *Imperial Rome and Christian Triumph* (1998).

THE LANGUAGE OF IMAGES IN ROMAN ART

TONIO HÖLSCHER

TRANSLATED BY
ANTHONY SNODGRASS AND
ANNEMARIE KÜNZL-SNODGRASS

WITH A FOREWORD BY
JAŚ ELSNER

CAMBRIDGE
UNIVERSITY PRESS

PUBLISHED BY THE PRESS SYNDICATE OF THE UNIVERSITY OF CAMBRIDGE
The Pitt Building, Trumpington Street, Cambridge, United Kingdom

CAMBRIDGE UNIVERSITY PRESS
The Edinburgh Building, Cambridge, CB2 2RU, UK
40 West 20th Street, New York, NY 10011–4211, USA
477 Williamstown Road, Port Melbourne, VIC 3207, Australia
Ruiz de Alarcón 13, 28014 Madrid, Spain
Dock House, The Waterfront, Cape Town 8001, South Africa

http://www.cambridge.org

Originally published in German as *Römische Bildsprache als semantisches System*
by Carl Winter Universitätsverlag Heidelberg, 1987

First published in English by Cambridge University Press 2004 as English translation

Printed in the United Kingdom at the University Press, Cambridge

Typeface Monotype Fournier 12.5/14 pt. *System* LaTeX 2ε [TB]

A catalogue record for this book is available from the British Library

ISBN 0 521 66200 1 hardback
ISBN 0 521 66569 8 paperback

The publication of this work was subsidized by a grant from
GOETHE-INSTITUT INTER NATIONES, Bonn.

Contents

Plates

Preface

The main lines of argument in this essay were first presented in a paper to the Heidelberger Akademie der Wissenschaften, and later formed the subject of lectures in various Universities, Archaeological Institutes and academic study groups. In the ensuing discussions, they were advanced by contributions, in particular, from J. Assmann, A. H. Borbein, F. Coarelli, H. Gabelmann, L. Giuliani, N. Himmelmann, St. Lehmann, E. Lefèvre, W. Schluchter, S. Settis, M. Torelli and P. Zanker. At the Archaeological Institute, Heidelberg I have been able to discuss the subject-matter above all with D. Grassinger, P. Karanastassis, C. Maderna-Lauter, H. G. Martin and St. Schröder, whose dissertations also deal in part with these questions. In the concluding stages of the work A. Dihle, who read the manuscript and improved it considerably with critical comments and suggestions, was of particular help to me. For the provision of illustrations, I was assisted by Archivi Alinari, M. Bertoletti, Hirmer Fotoarchiv, H. Jung, U. Kreilinger, N. Kunisch, H. Oehler, Th. Schäfer, S. L. Touati, H. Vögele. To them all, I owe cordial thanks.

Preface to the English edition

It is with particular pleasure that I see this book being published in a translation for an English-speaking audience. During the last ten years I have been introduced by the friendship of various scholars to the stimulating scene of Classical Studies in England as well as in the United States where I was challenged, by colleagues as well as by students, to open up my scholarly approaches to many new perspectives. Therefore, this English translation is first of all an act of gratitude. On the other hand, it has become more and more evident in recent times that scholarly orientations in the various countries are not only dramatically diverging – which in itself would not be problematic and could even be most fruitful – but that the multiplicity of approaches only rarely results in a productive pluralism since scholarly discourses tend more and more to isolate themselves within the boundaries of language. Translations can never compensate for the knowledge of foreign languages – on the contrary, they should encourage the acquisition of this knowledge.

The first suggestion of publishing an English version of this essay came from Emmanuele Curti, who aroused the interest of Cambridge University Press and stimulated influential colleagues to support this plan. Pauline Hire of Cambridge University Press was an indefatigable and encouraging driving force in long and difficult phases. An absolute stroke of luck was when Annemarie and Anthony Snodgrass were persuaded to undertake the translation which they did with wonderful insight and understanding. Afterwards Jaś Elsner contributed his very thoughtful introduction to my rather German approach into the intellectual scenery of the English-speaking world. Last but not least, the tiresome task of editing was taken over with enormous patience by Michael Sharp with the help of Sinéad Moloney. The translation was financed by Inter Nationes, Bonn. To all of them I express my deepest gratitude.

Foreword

By JAŚ ELSNER

Tonio Hölscher's essay, *The Language of Images in Roman Art*, is one of the most important and least well-known books (at least to an English-speaking readership) to have been published on Roman art in the past thirty years. Hölscher's formidable achievement is not only to have produced a wonderfully flexible and new theoretical understanding of Roman art, but to have grounded it – with a rare mixture of minute expertise and wide-ranging panache – in a careful discussion of the monuments themselves. Moreover, by returning art-historical and archaeological discussion to the age-old issues of style and form, Hölscher has breathed new life into a kind of art history many have left for dead. He is quite right to argue that we can only abandon questions of form – questions at the centre of every art-historical debate in Classical archaeology before the present generation – at our peril, not only since the methods of formalism are those by which objects have always been assessed and understood, but also because – if it loses its empathetic closeness to objects – art history risks heading into a tailspin ungrounded by any basis in material culture. Yet his is not a dry or antiquarian return to stylistic art history for its own sake. Rather, he has succeeded in uniting the great formalist strengths of the German tradition (of which he is one of the major living exponents) with a more recent interest in content and within the umbrella-theory of art as a linguistic system. In this union of old and modern approaches, he has created something genuinely new – both on the level of understanding Roman art and also as a theoretical postulate for the ways images more generally work as semantic vehicles for communication.

Although he gestures briefly to academic disciplines outside Classical archaeology and formalist art history, notably in the direction of semiotics and linguistics, Hölscher's theoretical contribution is grounded firmly in a precise analysis of monuments. Unlike much of the grand theory that has swept the human sciences (and especially art history) in the Anglo-American tradition since the 1980s,[1] Hölscher's is a theoretical approach built empirically from careful examination of objects within the constraints (but equally building upon the strengths) of a long German set of interrogations of this material. It is not theory applied to works of art, to see how far one can get, but rather a theoretical model derived from them. The fact that Hölscher's book may not look like art theory as one might expect it in Britain or the United States does not make his contribution any less theoretical or interesting. While German art-historical scholarship has a general tendency towards abstraction (something deeply embedded in its Kantian and Hegelian roots), this does not always go hand in hand with close theoretical reasoning. In its own context, Hölscher's work offers an outstanding example of abstraction built upon the foundations of a methodologically rigorous and theoretically astute empiricism.

The book is terse and closely argued. It is also strikingly reticent about its historiographic roots within German art-historical writing. For this reason it seems only fair to give the English reader a sense of its depth and significance beyond the ostensible objects and discussions presented in the book's substance. For Hölscher writes within a great theoretical tradition of art history, rocked to be sure by the crises of the first half of the last century,[2] but still vibrant enough to have produced (at the Classical end of art history alone) such dominant post-war voices as those of Nikolaus Himmelmann, Erika Simon and Paul Zanker as well as Hölscher's own.[3] This book is an active engagement with that tradition – not just archaeological but art-historical in its widest sense.[4] It is no surprise that, among the few Great Names Hölscher mentions, are a number – especially Panofsky and Wölfflin – who are not Classicists, but rather represent the finest theoretical reflections of the German art-historical tradition on the general questions of form and meaning which govern this book. In this sense, the author's contribution has ramifications well beyond Classical art history. For, although Hölscher's specific subject may be the relations of Roman art to its Greek roots and models, his deeper theme is a novel approach to the alignment of meaning (iconographic, iconological, social and contextual) with form (understood both as style and as a semantic system for using earlier visual types). And this issue – the ways form determines, defines, enables meaning – is one of the fundamental problems that characterise the entire German-speaking tradition of art history.

At the same time, Hölscher confronts head-on one of the oldest (and least resolved) chestnuts in the history of Classical art, the theme that Otto Brendel presented in 1953 as 'the Problem of Roman Art'. Hölscher's book may be described as the most comprehensive and satisfying general theory of Roman image-making since Brendel – to whom Hölscher is clearly and explicitly indebted – advanced his vastly influential, if obscurely entitled, *Prolegomena to the Study of Roman Art*, which was originally written in the early 1950s and has been required reading (especially in the United States) since its publication as a book in 1979.[5] One might say that as a thesis on how Roman images work in their cultural context, Hölscher's book replaces that of Brendel, whose conclusions on pluralism (pp. 122–37) were effectively a statement of his own position. It is the major theoretical contribution since Brendel's book and the eloquent Marxist reformulation of 'dualism' in Roman art proposed by Ranuccio Bianchi Bandinelli.[6] While there are several ways the field has moved on since the original German publication of this book,[7] there has certainly been no overarching attempt to summarise how and to explain why Roman art became the phenomenon it became, other than Hölscher's outstanding essay. Nor has there been any sustained engagement with the issues of form on anything like the scale which Hölscher achieves.

As a specifically historical contribution, Hölscher limits his thesis of 'art as a semantic system' to the uses of Greek prototypes within Roman art. However, his observations about the ways Romans appropriated external models can be extended to other artistic influences in Roman culture – notably, what scholars have labelled the native 'Italic' elements in Roman art (descending in part from Etruscan influence) and also non-Greek cultural appropriations into Rome – for instance (in both painting and sculpture) the adoption of Egyptiana. These visual forms (the 'Italic' often characterised by a radical rejection of the illusionistic conventions of scale and perspective normal in Roman art, and the Egyptian by Pharaonic and Ptolemaic styles) may be said to perform 'semantic' visual duties within Roman art on a basis exactly analogous to the Classicism explored by Hölscher. There can hardly be a greater compliment to a theoretical model than the observation that it can be satisfyingly extended. Moreover, in a period the book scarcely touches upon, Hölscher's postulate of the typological nature of the Roman language of images helps to explain aspects of the transformation of Roman art in late antiquity towards the art forms typical of the Middle Ages. If Hölscher is right about 'semantic' juxtaposition of types as a key to Roman image-making, then the eclecticism of late antique art – with its juxtapositions not of replicas resembling earlier prototypes but of actual examples culled from earlier periods in Roman art (the so-called practice of spoliation, of which the Arch of Constantine is the most famous example)[8] – is effectively a transformed continuation of Hölscher's semantics. While it is true that the Romans always borrowed (often stole!) actual examples of Greek art as well as its forms, types and styles, in late antiquity they transferred this process to their own earlier productions. All this is to say that, not only in the linguistic model of typological borrowings and semantic uses, but also in some of the specifically historical entailments of this model for late antique art, Hölscher's thesis seems not only sound but flexible enough to be enriched by the addition of further data outside his immediate sphere of concern.

Moreover, because the 'Classicism' of Roman art – its assimilation of and play with earlier models – is this essay's main subject, Hölscher's book plugs into a series of significant debates on the issues of cultural influence, borrowings and appropriation.[9] The question of the reception of earlier forms and visual paradigms is one that is not only fundamental to Roman art history, but is cardinal to the aesthetics of postmodernism itself – that period whose inception coincided directly with the writing of the book.[10] Hölscher's theory of Roman art may thus be seen to offer a historical paradigm on the visual level for some of the eclectic strategies and pick-and-mix genuflections of postmodernist art itself.

In what follows, I shall try to outline in a little more detail something of the art-historical traditions in which Hölscher's book should be situated. Besides providing a certain amount of historiographic and methodological background, this will – I hope – help to show the importance of Hölscher's specific contribution, as well as placing it in its own cultural context.

ROMAN ART

The two Roman art historians of an earlier generation whom Hölscher mentions by name in his introduction are Otto J. Brendel and Peter H. von Blanckenhagen. Hölscher cites them as his precursors in emphasising the pluralism of Roman image-making (p. 3). However, Brendel's book in particular is important to him as an earlier attempt to do some of the things Hölscher is attempting himself. Its strongly historiographic streak (it is in fact the major work of historiography in Roman art)[11] allows Hölscher largely to avoid the historiographic side of his subject and to tackle the visual material directly, without too much genuflection to earlier approaches. Yet the circumstances governing both Brendel's and Blanckenhagen's work are interesting in relation to their influence on Hölscher. Both were educated in the great German tradition before the Second World War; though neither was Jewish (Brendel being a clergyman's son and Blanckenhagen a Latvian nobleman from a family which fled from Russia to Germany to escape the Bolshevik revolution) both chose to leave Germany for America (Brendel before the War and Blanckenhagen after it), where both eventually settled in New York. Indeed, the very need for Brendel's book was surely motivated by his American experience.[12] His American students had neither the deep knowledge of the German tradition nor a suitable command of the German language to immerse themselves in what must have seemed the most recondite (and enormous) of formalist bibliographies. What was needed therefore was his own guide through that literature, worked up from a lecture published in Italian in the 1930s and completed with a more recent statement of where the field currently stood (as of 1953).[13] That Brendel himself represented the apogee of the tradition he was examining is perhaps inevitable (if not entirely modest!) – but it is an important warning to modern readers of the *Prolegomena* about the care with which one must handle its purported objectivity. It is ironic how important for those (like Hölscher) still within the German tradition is this somewhat slanted insider's portrait designed as an outsider's introduction.[14]

In the *Prolegomena*, Brendel asks two questions which not only govern his own discussion[15] but linger still to inform that of Hölscher. First, he worries as to whether there really was such a thing as Roman art with its own identity and value.[16] The classic Viennese intervention of the late nineteenth century, in the form of works by Franz Wickhoff (1853–1909) and Alois Riegl (1858–1905), had sufficiently affirmed the independent existence and value of Roman art,[17] but had left open the second of Brendel's questions – namely, 'What is Roman about Roman art?'[18] The post-Rieglian tradition of Roman archaeology might be described as a series of attempts to provide a solution. Some proposals, in the context of the rise of Nazism, were nationalistic and downright racist – an issue to which Hölscher alludes obliquely in chapter 2, when he criticises the 'absolute conception of individuality [as] applied not just to persons but to whole peoples'. In the years before and after the Second World War, a series of what Brendel characterises as 'dualistic' theories of Roman art were formulated, associated with such luminaries of the discipline as Gerhardt Rodenwaldt (1886–1945), Ranuccio Bianchi Bandinelli (1900–75) and Guido Kaschnitz-Weinberg (1890–1958).[19] These effectively divided Roman art into a great battle between the stylistic traits indigenous to Italy (variously described as anti-classical, Italic or Plebeian) and those borrowed from the Greeks. In English and American circles, by far the most influential of these dualisms was that proposed by Bianchi Bandinelli – who allied the dialectic of styles to a Marxist-influenced account of Plebeian (i.e. indigenous and Italic) versus Patrician (i.e. imported Hellenic) tendencies in Roman art.[20] In Germany, probably the most significant approach was the attempt to bridge stylistic dualism through an alternation of 'archaic', 'classical' and 'baroque' styles, argued by Rodenwaldt especially in his 1935 booklet on stylistic transformation as the motor for understanding historical change in Roman art.[21] It is this literature which Hölscher takes on in his second chapter, when he makes the incisive point that the obsession with stylistic exclusivity ultimately meant that the precise nature of the debts to earlier art within Roman image-making has remained unexplored, and in his third chapter, when he dismisses the notion of alternating styles. The position outlined by Brendel himself at the end of the *Prolegomena* was of a pluralism of styles – even on individual monuments (famous examples being the so-called Altar of Domitius Ahenobarbus from late Republican times and the Column Base of Antoninus Pius from the mid-second century AD). This was effectively only a version of the dualistic model, but the notion of pluralism – found also in Blanckenhagen's very early work on Flavian reliefs (a subject on which Hölscher is himself an expert)[22] – was to prove useful to Hölscher's rethinking of the entire problem.[23] The radicalism of Hölscher's position needs to be emphasised in an English-speaking context, where many of these debates seem far away. Many modern scholars still affirm a dualist or bipolar account of Roman art, of the sort that Hölscher is attacking.[24]

The Language of Images in Roman Art is thus much more deeply embedded in the traditional German debates of Roman art history than a cursory glance might lead one to imagine. It is an attempt within the discourse of a discipline centred on the German tradition though with key non-German interventions from Scandinavia and Italy (Brendel being ironically a rare English voice and Bianchi Bandinelli a seminal Italian one)[25] to resolve the problem of the Romanness of Roman art by tackling not its styles (as had the post-Rieglian tradition) but its 'semantic' or 'linguistic' methods of putting images together. This is a brilliant move, and it works. Someone who did not accept any of the premisses on which style art history is constructed might well not be convinced, since Hölscher's project is highly traditional in its acceptance of methodologies developed over more than a century. But given its constraints, and given some acceptance of 'style' and 'form' as proper provinces of art-historical research, what Hölscher offers is a view of Roman art as an unusual, highly sophisticated and in some ways very modern cultural system. It plays with earlier models (admittedly according to a series of rules or conventions which developed over time without necessarily being consciously formulated). In this regard,

Hölscher's theory of Roman image-making is highly museological in that there was clearly some awareness of the different pasts being evoked (through formal and stylistic features), as well as a willingness to undercut their pastness in a play of juxtaposition and combination. As with the collected works of different cultures in a modern museum, Roman art's evocation of different visual types from a variety of previous cultures elides the pastness of the past in a contemporaneity of display.[26]

FORMALIST ART HISTORY

When an acquaintance greets me on the street by lifting his hat, what I see from a formal point of view is nothing but the change of certain details within a configuration forming part of the general pattern of colour, lines and volumes that constitutes my world of vision. When I identify, as I automatically do, this configuration as an object (gentleman), and the change of detail as an event (hat lifting), I have already overstepped the limits of purely formal perception, and entered a first sphere of subject-matter or meaning.

So begins the second paragraph of Erwin Panofsky's introduction to his classic volume *Studies in Iconology*, first published in 1939.[27] The particular importance of this introduction lies in its elegant and consistent formulation of the place of iconology – the analysis of an object's range of meanings within its culture – in relation to iconography (the study of its content or subject-matter) and form (the exploration of the way it looks).[28] Hölscher refers directly to Panofsky's explorations of iconography and iconology (and hence probably to this piece) in his own first paragraph – explicitly for the fact that Panofsky never rejected the formalist side of visual studies so powerfully established in the German tradition.[29] In Anglo-American art history (at any rate before the great influx of German *émigrés* into the discipline in the States in the 1930s), formalism in the form of stylistic analysis had been primarily a matter of the connoisseurial identification of the individual styles of artists, and the concomitant interrelating of these artists into schools.[30] Such connoisseurial practice is associated above all with the brilliant identifications of hands by the American art historian Bernard Berenson (1865–1959),[31] for the Renaissance, and by the British Classical archaeologist Sir John Beazley (1885–1970),[32] for Attic vase-painting, and is dependent on the analytic method formulated by Giovanni Morelli (1816–1891).[33] By contrast, in the German tradition – to which Panofsky (who was one of the giants of German art history forced into American exile by Nazi persecution) is referring in the quotation above – form and style had a rather different significance. Following the attempts to write a cultural history using stylistic interrelations within a given epoch by scholars such as Jacob Burckhardt, Riegl and Wölfflin, the German tradition had focussed not so much on individual style as on 'period' or 'temporal' or 'collective' style as offering a series of social and historical facts identified by art-historical analysis and then usable as evidence in a broader historical argument. It is undoubtedly to this sense of style and form that Hölscher refers when arguing in his introduction that neglecting style is an unnecessary closing off of a range of valuable socio-historical evidence,[34] and subsequently when he talks of the ways Romans identified and used Greek period styles for their own purposes.

However, as my quotation from *Studies in Iconology* makes clear, what Hölscher also borrows implicitly from Panofsky is an interest in art as *communication* (beyond the lifting of hats) that combines questions both of form and of subject-matter. Like Panofsky, Hölscher is attempting to use the techniques of formal analysis as well as the theoretical basis on which it was established in conjunction with a form-related approach to meaning, to take the formalist tradition in new directions. The boldness of his own gestures towards a semantic model for Roman art is in danger of being camouflaged by the highly traditional formal language in which his treatment of monuments is expressed.

Like the history of the discipline of Classical archaeology, that of art history as a whole has not yet been (perhaps we should hope will never be!) authoritatively written. As with Brendel's *Prolegomena*, a number of the attempts cannot be read as anything but highly partisan clarion calls from participants in the project.[35] As with his treatment of the historiography of Roman art, Hölscher leaves a great deal unsaid about where he situates himself within the tradition to which he alludes by reference to Panofsky. His only other explicit historiographic references are an aside in chapter 2 about Winckelmann, the father of both art history and Classical archaeology, whose work represented the first systematic history of Greek art and was crucial in making Classical art accessible to a non-aristocratic audience, and a genuflection in chapter 3 to Wölfflin, who invented the notion of 'period' style.[36] Hölscher's discussion of period style in his third chapter is interesting, since – although it is grounded in the issue of Roman borrowings from Greek art – its presuppositions are much broader. He rejects the notion of Roman Classicism as itself a set of temporal styles within Rome appropriating the characteristic styles of different periods of Greek art in a systematic alternation of 'classical' and 'baroque' trends. Instead, he wants the borrowings to be rooted not in formal or stylistic options (or indeed in temporal changes of taste) but in choices of subject-matter. The specific forms chosen throughout the history of Roman art are selected, according to Hölscher's thesis, to communicate meanings in semantic units and structures. But, nevertheless, Hölscher accepts general style both in terms of particular ways of working marble which did change (or evolve) diachronically through Roman history, and also in terms of the periods of Greek art whose forms the Romans adopted. Again, what is clear here is a very careful positioning within the constraints of a deep academic dialogue conducted within the German tradition. Whether this positioning is consciously formulated or unconsciously imbibed through a lifetime's education, the most significant aspect for our purposes is a much more serious concern with the problems of style and form as a means of writing history than has been the case in Anglo-American art history or Classical archaeology since the 1980s.

THE SEMANTIC SYSTEM

Hölscher's solution to the 'Romanness' of Roman art is to emphasise the Romanness (despite its late Hellenistic origins) of the 'semantic system' by which the typical forms of different period styles in Greek art were adopted as types with specific meanings and manipulated in new ways (see especially chapter 8). This has resonances with linguistic and semiotic theories that became so sweepingly applied to the visual arts in the Anglo-American tradition at about the same time (that is, the early1980s when the book was conceived and the late 1980s when it was published).[37] In particular, Hölscher was influenced by the German translation of Umberto Eco's *La struttura assenta*, to which he explicitly refers in an important 1980 article on Roman art which anticipates some aspects of his thinking in *The Language of Images in Roman Art*.[38] In a brief autobiographical piece published in 1983, moreover, Hölscher signals his specific interest in theories of communication.[39] The notion of the 'semantic system' allows Hölscher to extend the linguistic metaphor to the 'paratactic' nature of Roman friezes (in chapter 7, for instance) and to present Roman art as primarily a visual culture of ideas, in which the forms and types are not only associated with the communication of meanings but acquire a hierarchical significance dependent on the culture's hierarchy of values (chapter 8). In all this, the language image and the notion of semantics act as a powerful metaphor for the process Hölscher is describing. But the idea of the 'semantic system', too, should be seen as motivated by and profoundly embedded in the German art-historical tradition, operating as something more fundamental than a mere metaphor.[40]

In the 1890s, Riegl – the only great scholar who figures with as much distinction in the history of art history as he does in that of Classical archaeology – had produced successive manuscripts for a book entitled *A Historical Grammar for the Visual Arts*. This remained unpublished at his untimely death in 1905, only saw the light in the 1960s and has never been translated into English.[41] In an academic tradition where form acquired the independent historical and socio-cultural significance accorded to it by the Austrians and Germans, and even – in the neo-Hegelian developments of Riegl – a kind of will of its own,[42] the structural and specifically linguistic interpretation of art became hard to resist. In the 1930s, for instance, there were distinguished attempts by such scholars as the Renaissance specialist Julius von Schlosser (1866–1938) – the great Viennese teacher of Pächt, Kris, Kurz, Ladner and Gombrich among others – specifically to explore the structural parallels of stylistic and linguistic models for the visual arts.[43] The Viennese-trained Classical archaeologist Guido Kaschnitz-Weinberg wrote an important 'structuralist' account of early Italian art in 1933,[44] one of its author's series of examinations of the structure of ancient art,[45] which occasioned a fierce polemic on precisely the issue of the linguistic parallel from Bianchi Bandinelli.[46]

Ultimately, there may be more than one way to read Hölscher's convergence of language and artistic form. One might argue that the forms of Roman art (though not their specific handling by artists at different times) are *stripped* of specifically stylistic significance and relegated (to use Hölscher's own word, but one might equally say 'elevated') to the sphere of semantic expression. A second approach may be to say that the visual appearance or style of works of art has certain language-like (Hölscher's term is 'semantic') properties, such as structure and organisation, but that it still communicates through the sensuous means of form, and thus carries with it some specific entailments of form as elaborated above all by the German tradition of style art history. The difference between these two interpretations lies in how one understands the relationship between signs and what they signify. Is the meaning given to signs (including the visual arts) only a matter of prevailing cultural convention at different times or is it in some sense intrinsically related to and even essentially encoded in the signs which communicate that meaning (for instance, the *sound* of words or the *sensual properties* of visual forms)? Hölscher's book is not explicit about this issue, but in the letter he wrote to me in response to the first draft of this introduction he mentions his serious problems with the essentialism underlying the formal 'structuralism' of the Vienna School.[47] This is not in itself a full endorsement of the first of the two interpretations suggested here, but it certainly distances itself from the second. This, however, is one of those areas where perhaps readers might take over from the author (and his various interpreters), and develop their own positions on one of the key questions of how art – and indeed all cultural signs – communicate.

The fact that *The Language of Images in Roman Art* is deeply indebted to Hölscher's own historiographic tradition should not blind us to its originality. Like the very Roman art which Hölscher discusses, his own book is deeply imbued with the intellectual strategies and theoretical models of the past. But its originality – like that of the finest examples of

Roman art – lies in how expertly it plays with those typologies, transforming familiar monuments and familiar art-historical terminology (familiar at least to those bred in the German tradition!) to new ends and innovative arguments. The result is something very like the best Roman art in Hölscher's own account – a deep analysis, conscious of what it borrows (even if not always explicit about it) but novel in how it redistributes the elements it has inherited, convincing in the way it makes those elements its own and compelling as an interpretative picture of Roman art for our time.

NOTES (For further reading, see pp. 141–7 below)

I am grateful to Tonio Hölscher, Natalie Boymel Kampen, Rolf Schneider, Michael Sharp and Jeremy Tanner for their very helpful comments on the first draft of this foreword.

1. See for a general account e.g. Skinner (1985). For art history, see for instance among a plethora of recent titles, Bryson *et al.* (1991); Melville and Readings (1995); Cheetham *et al.* (1998).
2. A full history has yet to be written. For an outstanding account of the politics of Classical archaeology (focussing on philhellenic rather than Roman interests, and largely excluding that significant part of the German-speaking tradition which hailed from what was once Austria-Hungary rather than Germany proper), see Marchand (1996), esp. 228–368.
3. In a brief autobiographical piece published on the occasion of his election to the Heidelberg Academy, Hölscher reports that he owes his interest in Roman art to the influence of Erika Simon. See Hölscher (1983), 29–33, esp. 30. I am very grateful to Rolf Schneider for sending me his copy of this piece.
4. For Hölscher's own brief comments on post-war German Classical archaeology, see Hölscher (1983) 31–2.
5. Brendel (1979). 'The Problem of Roman Art' is the title of the first chapter, p. 3. See also Bianchi Bandinelli (1936).
6. For Bianchi Bandinelli's work in this area, see for instance, Bianchi Bandinelli (1970), esp. 51–106 and Bianchi Bandinelli (1978a), 19–78, as well as Bianchi Bandinelli (1979). For some other theoretical contributions in English, in addition to the (mainly German) bibliography cited by Hölscher himself, see for instance Vogel (1968) and Nodelman (1993) (first published in 1975).
7. Among the developments have been the brilliant analysis of the relations of art and power in Rome by Zanker (1988) (published in German in the same year as Hölscher's book in 1987); an increasingly deep understanding of the sociological nature of Roman images (for instance Gregory (1994) and Tanner (2000)); a particular interest in problems of sexuality and gender (see

for example the edited collections of Kampen (1996) and Koloski-Ostrow and Lyons (1997) and a renewed focus on issues of spectatorship (see for example Elsner (1995); Zanker (1997); Bergmann and Kondoleon (1999)).

8. Spoliation is a big topic, especially in German art history. In English, see the fine recent articles by Kinney (1995) and Kinney (1997) with further bibliography. On the Arch of Constantine, see Elsner (2000), with bibliography.
9. See, for example, Nelson (1996); Cutler (1996); Zerner (1997); the essays in Payne *et al.* (2000); and specifically on Laokoön (the supreme ancient statue with a modern afterlife) Settis (1999) and Brilliant (2000).
10. See, for example, Foster (1983); Kaplan (1988); Brooker (1992); Bhabha (1996).
11. However, see also Bianchi Bandinelli (1978b), 117–67 for a more methodologically orientated twentieth-century historiography of Roman art.
12. For an important discussion of the Americanness of the *Prolegomena* in the era of McCarthyism, see Kampen (1997). Kampen makes the point that the very 'pluralism' upheld by Hölscher, which Brendel claims as his own contribution (along with other scholars like Hinks, Blanckenhagen and Hamberg, Brendel (1979) 122–37), belongs quite specifically within the discourse of the United States during McCarthyism.
13. The 1930s lecture is Brendel (1936), republished in Brendel (1982) 3–20; the original publication of the *Prolegomena* was in Brendel (1953).
14. For some discussion of Brendel's position, see Bianchi Bandinelli (1961/1979) 234–58, esp. 235–8; Settis (1982) and Denti (1985). On the problems of writing a history of Roman art, see Kampen (1995).
15. See Kampen (1997) 383.
16. Brendel (1979) 4–9. For a sensitive and historiographically commanding review of the problem, that postdates the original publication of Hölscher's book and applies some of its findings, see Settis (1989).
17. See F. Wickhoff's contribution to Ritter von Härtel and Wickhoff (1895) (translated by E. Strong as Ritter von Härtel and Wickhoff (1900)) and Riegl (1901) (translated by R. Winkes as Riegl (1985)). There are several discussions of this literature in English, not least that of Brendel (1979) 25–37, but also Olin (1992), 129–53 and Iversen (1993), 71–90.
18. Brendel (1979) 9, 41.
19. Brendel's account is in (1979) 101–21; see also Settis (1989) 833–41.
20. See Bianchi Bandinelli (1970) and Bianchi Bandinelli (1971). Clearly Bianchi Bandinelli's influence on Hölscher was significant. The latter spent a year in Rome as a student under the supervision of Bianchi Bandinelli, to whom he attributes the grounding of his understanding of art theory: see Hölscher (1983) 30.

21. See Rodenwaldt (1935), esp. 25 7.
22. Von Blanckenhagen (1942); Hölscher (1992).
23. Most recently on pluralism, see Settis (1989) 823–63.
24. For a recent restatement of 'bipolarity', see Torelli (1996), 930–1, 956–8. For an interesting account of the ways the Greek/indigenous version of bipolarity has governed the historiography of a single monument, see Conlin (1997), 11–25.
25. On the English side, we should not forget Hamberg (1945) (to which Hölscher refers several times). This is the work of a Swedish scholar whose engagement (like Brendel's) is almost entirely with the German tradition. One suspects that it would have been published in German and not English, had Hamberg's reaction to contemporary history (what he calls 'circumstances only too well known', p. 6) not diverted him.
26. Museology is a field that has radically 'taken off' in Britain and America since Hölscher first wrote this book. For some significant collections of essays, see Vergo (1989) and Karp and Lavine (1991); also Crimp (1993) and for some specifically art-historical pieces, Preziosi (1998).
27. Panofsky (1962), 3 (this introduction was revised in 1955 as 'Iconography and Iconology' in Panofsky (1957), 26–54).
28. For a brief account of these distinctions, see Lash (1996), 89–98. Frankly, I myself think the distinction is not entirely free of woolliness. In his 1955 rewriting of the introduction, Panofsky substituted the term 'iconology' (1957, p. 31) for what he called in 1939 (in italics) '*iconography in a deeper sense*' (1962, p. 8). In parentheses added to the 1939 version he wrote in 1955: 'I conceive of iconology as an iconography turned interpretative and thus becoming an integral part of the study of art instead of being confined to the role of a preliminary survey' (1957, p. 32), but nonetheless admitted the danger that 'iconology will behave, not like ethnology as opposed to ethnography, but like astrology as opposed to astrography' (1957, p. 32). Accordingly, when he then used the term 'iconological interpretation' in his 1955 revision (1957, p. 38) to replace his 1939 formulation 'the interpretation of the *intrinsic meaning or content*, dealing with what we have termed "*symbolical values*" instead of *images, stories and allegories*' (1962, p. 14, his italics), one wonders whether astrology rather than ethnology had not already taken over in 1939 and was being covered up by a convenient but actually rather meaningless shorthand.
29. On Panofsky's relations with formalism – especially in his theoretically more creative German period before emigration to the United States – see Alpers (1979), esp. 104–6; Holly (1984), 46–96; Wood (1991); Iversen (1993) 149–66.

30. For some useful introductions to style, see Schapiro (1994), 51–102; Ackerman (1963), 164–86; Gombrich (1968); Sauerländer (1983); Davis (1990); Elsner (2003). Specifically on individual style, see Wollheim (1979) and Wollheim (1995), esp. 40–6.
31. On Berenson's connoisseurship, see Berenson (1902) and Berenson (1927), with, for example, Calo (1993) and the attack of Schapiro (1994) 209–26.
32. On Beazley, see Kurtz (1985); Neer (1997); Whitley (1997).
33. On Morelli, see Wind (1985) 30–46; Wollheim (1973) 177–201; Ginzburg (1983); Maginnis (1990); Zerner (1997) 15–34.
34. This is a position recent Anglo-American sociology of art would support: see Witkin (1995), 5–15, esp. 12–13; likewise the most recent major study in the anthropology of art, see Gell (1998), 155–220 (though Gell finds the art-historical formulation of 'style', which he accesses through the work of Wollheim, one 'we probably cannot make anthropological use of', p. 156).
35. For example, Belting (1987) (originally published in German in 1983); Pächt (1999) (originally published in German in 1986). Perhaps the most balanced general account is Podro (1982).
36. For Wölfflin on general style, see Wölfflin (1950) 6–17. A useful critique (indeed a rejection of the concept) is Wollheim (1995) esp. 46–8.
37. See, for instance, Bal and Bryson (1991) with a rich bibliography. Of course, I do not mean here to imply that semiotics was *new* to art history in the 1980s. For a much older tradition of its application, see the famous essay by Schapiro (1969) in Schapiro (1994) 1–32.
38. See Hölscher (1980a), esp. 267, n.7. Eco's *La struttura assenta: La ricerca semiotica e il metodo strutturale*, Milan, 1968 was translated into German as *Einführung in die Semiotik*, Munich, 1972. Rolf Schneider, who was a student in Heidelberg in the 1970s, tells me that Hölscher's seminar at this period was much concerned with applying Eco's 'structuralism' to various types of Roman images.
39. See Hölscher (1983) 31: 'Kommunikationswissenschaft'.
40. For an anglophone philosophical exploration of the parallelism of art and language, see Wollheim (1980), esp. 104–58; and for some recent Anglo-American discussions, see the essays in Kemal and Gaskell (1991).
41. Riegl (1966). See Scarrocchia (1986) 68–74 and Olin (1992) 113–28.
42. See Zerner (1976), esp. 180–2 and Wood (1991), 7–16. For an early and acute American critique of this tradition, see Schapiro (1936).
43. Schlosser (1935) (published in Italian as Schlosser (1936)).
44. Kaschnitz-Weinberg (1933).
45. Conveniently collected in Kaschnitz-Weinberg (1965). For an interesting attempt to compare Kaschnitz's 'structuralism' with that of (his rough contemporary) Claude Lévi-Strauss, see Nodelman (1966). Until very recently,

none of Kaschnitz's work was translated into English, but see now his 'Remarks on the Structure of Egyptian Sculpture' (1933) in Wood (2000) 199–242. There is a long review of his work by Bieber (1967).

46. Bianchi Bandinelli (1937), esp. 191–2, with the response of Kaschnitz-Weinberg on pp. 280–4, and the riposte of Bianchi Bandinelli on pp. 284–6 of the same volume. See the discussions of this debate by Sedlmayr (1959), esp. 21–4 and Scarrocchia (1986) 145–9.
47. For an English opening to the Vienna School see the introduction and essays in Wood (2000). This is a very useful collection, but might be criticised for over-emphasising the so-called 'Second Vienna School' of the 1930s and underplaying the concerns with style art history and *Geistesgeschichte* of the previous two generations in Viennese art history.

Chronology of Greek art and artists

PERIODS/STYLES OF GREEK ART

Archaic	700–480 BC
Classical	480–330/300 BC
High Classical	450–430/420 BC
Hellenistic	330/300–30 BC
'Severe Style'	480–450 BC
'Rich Style'	430/420–400 BC

GREEK ARTISTS

	Active
Alkamenes	*ca.* 450–400 BC
Antiphilos	*ca.* 330–300 BC
Apelles	*ca.* 330–300 BC
Chares	*ca.* 300 BC
Damophon of Messene	First half of second century BC
Demetrios	Late fifth century BC
Kalamis	*ca.* 470–430 BC
Kallimachos	Late fifth century BC
Lysippos	*ca.* 375–315 BC
Myron	*ca.* 460–440 BC
Parrhasios	Late fifth century BC
Pasiteles	First half of first century BC
Pheidias	*ca.* 470–430 BC
Polykleitos	*ca.* 460–420 BC

Praxiteles	*ca.* 370–320 BC
Protogenes	*ca.* 330–300 BC
Timarchides	Second quarter of second century BC
Zeuxis	Late fifth century BC

Glossary

aemulatio ambitious emulation
aeternitas immortality
aretē (pl. *aretai*) goodness, excellence, virtue
atrium the first main room in a Roman-style house, where visitors were received
auctoritas (of gods, magistrates/leading persons) authority; (of works of art) impressiveness, dignity, authority
charis grace
clementia clemency
concordia concord, unanimity, solidarity
cura serious attention, care
decor appropriate adornment, appropriate beauty
dignitas standing, esteem, importance
diligentia carefulness, attentiveness
elegantia refinement
enargeia vividness, graphic clarity
ēthos character
exemplum an example (for imitation), model
facilitas facility, ease
felicitas good fortune, luck
flamen (pl. *flamines*) a Roman priest appointed to carry out the ritual of one particular deity
genus (pl. *genera*) style, mode of expression
genus floridum a flowery style, bright with rhetorical colour
genus robustum a mature style
genus subtile a precise, logical style, based on argument alone without appeal to the emotions

gratia agreeableness, charm
gravitas solemnity, majesty
hupsos sublimity, grandeur
imitatio producing a copy or imitation
ingenium skill, ingenuity
interpretatio translation
kallos beauty
kalokagathia the character and conduct of a perfect man, nobleness, goodness
labor toil, effort
leptotēs fineness, delicacy
magnificentia splendour, magnificence
maiestas majesty, grandeur
megaleios magnificent, splendid
megaloprepeia magnificence
megethos loftiness, sublimity
neoterics modern term applied to Catullus and a few like-minded contemporaries who aimed to apply the ideal of elegance and style represented by the Hellenistic Greek poet Kallimachos
nobilitas nobility
paideia learning, education
peripeteia sudden reversal of circumstances
phōs light
pietas an attitude of dutiful respect towards those to whom one is bound by ties of religion, consanguinity, matrimony, friendship, loyalty (to the state or a commander)
pondus gravity, dignity, solemnity
proceritas height, elongation
pulchritudo (*eximia*) beauty, attractiveness (outstanding)
sanctitas holy purity, sacred virtue
semnotēs solemnity, dignity
tablinum a room in a Roman house running between the *atrium* and the peristyle
veritas reality
virtus (pl. *virtutes*) manly spirit, valour

CHAPTER I

*Introduction**

My aim in this book is to examine the language of images in the art of the Roman Empire as an essential factor in Roman culture. Recent efforts to explore the political and social meanings of Roman figural art have tended to push issues of form and style into the background. By contrast, the problems of iconography and iconology have been emphasised – though the formulation of modern iconology by Erwin Panofsky (1892–1968) did not necessarily entail the one-sided implications of sidelining the significance of form.[†] Certainly, as new art-historical questions are being formulated, we can carry on for a while without recourse to the traditional methods and analyses grounded in formalism. But it is my proposition that the sacrifice of formal analysis has much more serious consequences than is often appreciated – especially for social history. For few cultural phenomena have a more pronounced collective and social character than artistic style and the language of artistic imagery.

The exploration of stylistic forms offers a way of measuring cultural identity – not just in the case of individuals but especially of larger groupings, including entire cultures and epochs. It is no accident that history as a whole has borrowed so many of its temporal and cultural subdivisions from the history of art. The units of space and time which may be defined by the *style* of a group, period or region bear witness to the social interconnections of the original exponents of that style. There is no space here to explore these questions further, but their bearing on history in general has by no means been exhausted.

Moreover, the common visual language of a society – underlying the thematics of its imagery and regardless of minor temporal and local stylistic differences – is a social fact of the greatest interest. Among the fundamental themes for social history raised by the communicative aspects of the history of images are the following: how a society may coin a means of visual communication, how this language then reacts upon the society as it uses and develops it, what the overall visual system is able to achieve as a result, which structures of meaning are implied in its syntax and repertoire of motifs. All these are of real importance for social and cultural history.

The attempt to clarify these issues can only be convincing if it can claim a certain degree of universal validity. Yet – in the case of Roman art – among the obstacles is the fact that so much of the evidence, especially of 'idealising' sculpture, has hardly been examined and set out in a systematic way. Of necessity, in a short account like this, the burden of proof must be borne by only a very few examples. Indeed, despite all efforts to represent a fairly balanced range of works, it remains true that no one can yet claim to have a complete overview of the whole field today. It is the familiar dilemma: if one looks at the whole before its parts, the picture risks being out of focus, even distorted; if one reverses the order, it loses any general structure, becoming a jumble of parts. To my mind, the latter is the greater risk. But at the same time I must admit that this book is only a first, rough sketch.

My project is to explore the language of imagery in Roman art as a semantic system. This 'semantic system' functions according to a sort of grammar, on the basis of certain specific structures (like a language). I mean a system in the broad sense – not a consistent structure shaped by unifying principles but a flexible interplay of elements which together form a co-ordinated whole. This visual language was not consciously devised. Rather it evolved gradually and organically. This means there was a considerable degree of inconsistency in its expression. One must be cautious, therefore, in deploying exceptional cases as arguments against the validity of the system as a whole. Since no culture was ever designed to fit to scientific measurements and methods of research, academic study must develop models and points of view which account for the indeterminacies of cultural life.

It is difficult to assess the extent of the validity of the semantic system I propose in the following pages. That the phenomena exist can hardly be doubted in the light of Roman documentary sources (some of which I shall examine below). But it is equally clear that there are exceptions to how far we can apply the structures of the system I shall discuss. The limits of my suggestions about the language of Roman art and the extent of their applicability are questions which future research must clarify. My sketch needs to be tested not only by a review of additional monuments; it must also be enlarged beyond its present margins. For a 'grammatical' system of visual language can never encompass all manifestations of art in a culture. It can only be set alongside other phenomena – for instance, temporal changes in style and various formal constraints, such as concepts of space and body. The semantic system presented here was inevitably mediated by the development of style and by such pre-linguistic structures of form as space and body, and my theoretical presentation of it needs to be filtered through a theorisation of these issues.

It is illuminating to compare the visual arts with other aspects of cultural production, above all with Roman literature and literary theory. Modern theory (I have linguistics and semiotics particularly in mind) is also helpful. I have profited from the awareness of these possibilities but confess that I am far from having exhausted them.

This essay is, in fact, a very preliminary and open-ended sketch. My aspiration is that it will be assessed, clarified and (let us hope) enriched by discussion and criticism, rather than that it be set in stone. Similar reflections have, on occasion, been offered before. Instead of overburdening the text with numerous scattered notes, I shall mention a few authors who have been particularly important for me. Of prime significance are the projects of Otto Brendel (1901–73) and Peter H. von Blanckenhagen (1901–90), who between them first pointed the way towards a pluralistic understanding of Roman art.[1] More recently, Paul Zanker has identified some characteristic features of the Roman language of images in his general sketch of Classicism in Roman Imperial culture. Likewise, Adolf H. Borbein has pursued similar questions in an unpublished lecture to the Mommsen-Gesellschaft, delivered at Würzburg in 1980.[2] Otherwise, my approach derives – more perhaps than I am consciously aware – from day-to-day life experience: the modern restriction of personal initiative in daily life by an overriding tendency towards cohesion and social collectivity seems to me to be becoming ever more oppressive.

NOTES

* Style of references: as in *Archäologischer Anzeiger* 1985, 757ff. Additionally, *Classicisme* = Fondation Hardt, *Entretiens sur l'antiquité classique* 25: *Le Classicisme à Rome aux* 1ers *siècles avant et après J.-C.* (1979).

† By contrast with the *form* and *style* of artworks, iconography is the study of their subjects and themes. Iconology is a broader analysis using the results of both iconographic and stylistic study to place a work of art in its full cultural context and hence to delineate its complex of meanings. [JE]

1. Brendel (1936); (1953); (1979). See also Settis (1982); Blanckenhagen (1942).
2. Zanker in *Classicisme*, 283–306. I myself, after prolonged preparation, first put forward these thoughts in a lecture at Münster in 1980. They represent an extension, to cover the language of imagery, of the phenomena which made up the Roman view of history (which in turn stand as proxies for a wide range of themes in Roman art), which are set out in Hölscher (1980a). For further references, see chapter 3, n.22 (p. 22).

CHAPTER 2

The Greek paradigm: a model for life-style, a case of academic classicism, or a building block of Imperial culture?

Roman works of art, with rare exceptions, correspond so little to modern ideas of 'creative art' that scholars have had to resort to an unusual array of theories in the effort to make sense of them. In one respect, at least, this is an advantage. Greek art, by contrast, readily arouses feelings of unmediated familiarity which seem universally valid and are as a result obstacles to understanding. Roman art, on the other hand, has always been handled at a distance, has only been made accessible by intellectual bridge-building. As a consequence, Classical art history has over the past century developed its most important tenets and theories in relation to Roman rather than Greek art.

These theoretical concepts have especially examined general issues of form, conceptions of space and the body, variations of style across time and artistic genre, as well as the problematics of function and the sociological conditions under which art has been created. However, surveying this set of conceptual investigations,[1] one is struck forcefully by the fact that one basic and fundamental element of Roman art – namely, the indelible stamp of Greece – has been largely ignored as a subject for theoretical reflection in its own right (although it has never been explicitly denied). This omission entails both premisses and consequences. At the heart of the matter lies the often unspoken demand for originality, which is defined as an absolute quality, confined to artistic forms and thus denied any concrete historical context. Closely linked with this is an equally absolute conception of individuality, applied not just to persons but to whole peoples. Originality is what guarantees the nature of 'Romanness' in its own right. In this context, 'Greek' and 'Roman' come to be terms of polar opposition.[2]

In so far as Roman art was indebted to Greek models, it could never satisfy this (modern) call for originality. Thus the question of its Greek foundations was taken as a given and lost its interest both for the positive and the negative commentators on Roman images. Johann Joachim Winckelmann (1717–68), for example, saw the dependence of Roman art on Greek models as the basis for making his dismissive judgment of a 'style of imitators'. Conversely, the positive re-evaluation of Roman art since the beginning of the twentieth century emphasised the independent and fruitful nature of Roman forms. Behind this opposing banner, however, art historians remained committed to the old call for originality. The effect was that the Greek elements within Roman image-making had to be declared a foreign disruption to the indigenous and independent genius of Roman art. The Greekness of Roman art was pushed aside as a secondary and marginal issue. Where Roman art had at first been of secondary rank *because of* its imitation of Greek styles, it was now significant *in spite of* its temporary domination by Greek styles. In effect, both these perspectives – their polar opposition notwithstanding – largely lost sight of what remains a crucial aspect of visual production in Rome: that is, the Greek roots of Roman art.

One consequence has been a unilateral and self-imposed constraint on scholarly discussion. Research has been devoted to those works of art which – individually or collectively – could be seen as particularly 'Roman'. Above all, this has meant a focus on portraiture – especially portraits from the Republic and from late antiquity; on the so-called 'historical reliefs' – especially those from Flavian and Trajanic times, or of popular art; and on certain fields within architecture. Other substantial classes of Roman figural images – for instance, idealising sculpture or mythological reliefs – have long been neglected, not only as subjects for theoretical study, but even as objects of systematic and definitive publication. Explicitly or implicitly, the 'classicising' factors in Roman art have been effectively declared obsolete. The measure of success in an artistic movement was the degree to which it distanced itself from the 'classical' forms of the Greek paradigm.[3]

This model of interpretation has, for some time, been losing its appeal.[4] It is beyond argument that Roman art, in each of its fields and in as many different ways, rests on Greek foundations. In particular, it is clear that by the late Republic Rome was in many ways a Graeco-Hellenistic metropolis,[5] and that many traditions of later Roman art go back to this period. It may be an oversimplification to see Roman image-making as no more than a continuation of Greek art,[6] but it is certainly wrong to regard its fundamental 'Romanness' as an autonomous structure of basic forms that are polar opposites to the forms of Greek art. The supposed antithesis of 'Greek' and 'Roman' art conceals a decisive and continuous historical process. At the same time, more nuanced understandings have opened us to the fact that some Roman works of art show particularly strong Greek influence.[7] Beyond this, the issue of Classicism itself has become an area of increasing discussion.[8]

A precondition for this new understanding of Roman art (to which my own work is intended as a contribution) is the rejection of certain premisses that have been taken as axiomatic. Above all, we must break free of the expectation of ceaseless innovation, often in the form of progressive 'development', and of the assumption that a unified, free-standing, style is somehow expressive of historical individuality.[9] But a further requirement is also necessary. We can no longer approach works of art exclusively from the standpoint of production, as the expressions of artists or patrons, but we must also examine them as forms of communication – that is, as a factor in the collective life of a society.[10] It is from this point that the present enquiry into the visual language of Roman art and its function in Roman culture will start. A culture – and even one of its branches, such as figural art – can only be meaningfully described as a system of all the elements belonging to it. Only when we grasp the historical function of the system as a whole can we begin to asess the importance of its component factors.

The problematic use of the term 'Classicism' itself exemplifies the difficulty of defining the relationship between Roman art and its Greek models.[11] In a narrow sense, we can use the term to indicate reference to paradigms from the 'Classical' period of Greek art (that is from the fifth and fourth centuries BC), giving special attention to the 'High Classical' decades of Pheidias and Polykleitos. On the other hand, 'Classicism' in a wider sense denotes the reception of Greek art as a whole, from the Late Archaic period down to the end of the Hellenistic. This is no mere terminological problem.

First, we must start from the fact that both these forms of reception actually exist. Next, we need to acknowledge that the conscious reference to the 'Classical period' in the narrower sense is a very different phenomenon from the all-embracing usage of different styles within the repertoire of Greek art. In the first case, we are offered a consistent intellectual attitude, a striving for scale and order, a programme – in short – that evokes 'timeless' values, establishes norms, eliminates conflicting attitudes and makes pedagogic demands.[12] In the second case, we find a response to the past that registers and refers eclectically to a variety of historical traditions, a response directed at a rather more diffuse educational ideal.

One might, at this stage, simply conclude that both traditions existed – appealing diversely to the moral ideologues, aiming at a specific goal, and to the educated public, with its range of broad-minded interests. Yet, between them, the definitions of these two forms of 'Classicism' address only part of the question. Neither of them succeeds in explaining why works of art in the Greek traditions achieved so vast a distribution, over the entire extent of the Roman Empire. Equally, the great bulk of Roman work recalls its Greek prototypes only in a very general (one might even say tired and artistically weak) form – thus responding neither to the demands of a higher enlightenment nor to those of a programmatic intellectual regime.[13] The broad population of the Empire consisted neither of backward-facing ideologues nor of trained art-historians – and yet this art won widespread approval. One might wonder therefore whether current explanations are not pitched at too high a level. Perhaps the visual language of Roman art had a more rudimentary set of functions for the general public as a whole.[14] This brings us to this question: what exactly *was* the achievement of the Greek tradition for Roman Imperial culture?

NOTES

1. For critical analysis see Brendel (1953) 9ff. and (1979) 3ff., 139ff.; Bianchi Bandinelli (1960) and (1979) 108ff.; Settis (1982) 161ff.
2. On this see Brendel (1979) 47ff., 68ff., and Settis (1982) 178.

3. On this see Sichtermann (1974).
4. Brendel (1979) 84ff. and Bianchi Bandinelli (1960) and (1979).
5. Thanks above all to the researches of F. Coarelli; for one representative example out of many, see Coarelli (1970–1). Important too is Zanker (1976).
6. Exemplified by Toynbee (1934), on which see the fundamental comments of Brendel (1979) 72ff.
7. Above all, in recent years, in the work of Zanker (1974).
8. e.g. Jucker (1950), Wünsche (1972) 45–80, Sichtermann (1974). Preisshofen and Zanker in *Classicisme*, 263–77 and 283–306 respectively.
9. For Roman art, this begins with Brendel (1936) 122ff. and (1979) 122ff. and Blanckenhagen (1942) 310–41. In practice, however, the phenomena of temporal styles have continued to attract much greater attention than the various more static factors in Roman art.
10. For an example of the aesthetic dominance of the categories of production and expression, see the (nonetheless stimulating) essay by Wünsche (1972). Compare n.14 below.
11. For an attempt to define this expression, without the distinction made here, see Gelzer in *Classicisme*, 1–41, esp. 10ff. More closely related to the phenomena under discussion, Zanker, *Classicisme*, 45, 299ff. In this work (to have done with the burden of terminology) I make very restricted use of the term 'Classicism': not for the aspects of typology, but only for stylistic attitudes (see pp. 11, 21 below), and then only for the programmatic concentration on fifth- and fourth-century BC models. But I am here concerned only with the phenomena: one might perfectly well give them different labels.
12. See most recently Gelzer in *Classicisme*, 1–41.
13. These features, among other questions, are given special emphasis by Zanker in *Classicisme*, 283ff.
14. This forms a fundamental ground for objection to the all-too-general use of the high-cultural, production-centred aesthetic categories of *interpretatio*, *imitatio* and *aemulatio* for Roman public sculpture by Wünsche (1972). They can have been valid for only a narrow range of thinking artists and viewers.

CHAPTER 3

The monuments: how the language works

At first sight, one might adopt a simple and consistent model for the reception of Greek prototypes in Roman art. Each succeeding epoch of Roman history might be presented as embracing a different phase of Greek art, in which a sympathetic stylistic ideal was identified and seized upon. Thus, in the Augustan period, the dominant type of imperial portrait witnesses a return to the orderly 'Classical' (in the narrow sense) language of the fifth century BC – especially that of Polykleitos.[1] In the Flavian period, by contrast, the portraits of Vespasian follow the colourful, 'baroque', formal language of Hellenistic art.[2] According to this model, these choices of specific prototypes are seen as representative of their respective epochs in Roman culture. A similar case can be made for the Classicism of the Hadrianic and the 'baroque' of the Antonine periods in the second century AD.

This model of Classicism will not do. It is based on an idea of the development of Roman art as a pendulum, swinging between classicising and baroque phases.[3] Classical and baroque are here understood, in the sense first proposed by Heinrich Wölfflin (1864–1945), to be polar opposites and – at the same time – temporal styles. These period styles of Roman art are defined by the conscious selection of specific period styles in Greek art. The very identity of the relevant Roman epoch finds its expression through the stylistic choices made in this way. Obviously, this way of seeing 'Classicism' is just an extension of the history constructed, though partly by different means, for Greek art.[4] That is, it is a story of a developing progression through fundamentally unitary temporal styles – though now no longer a process of independent innovation, but rather a series of selections from specimens of older exemplary styles.

But the application of this model to our evidential base of surviving monuments simply doesn't work. Close inspection of Roman art reveals a picture of bewildering diversity. In every period of Roman history, the most varied stylistic phases of Greek art – from Late Archaic to late Hellenistic – are picked up and exploited. The High Classical figure-type of Polykleitos from the mid-fifth century BC is the influence for the 'Idolino' in Florence (from the beginning of the Imperial period, plate 1).[5] But equally, a hundred years later in Flavian times, the same model is appropriated for the statue of a youth in the Vatican (plate 2).[6] Meanwhile, an Augustan altar in Arezzo, with the Roman She-wolf, the Twins and the Shepherds (plate 3), belongs to the tradition of mythological landscapes,[7] which was only developed in Hellenistic times. And yet this is equally true of a Flavian relief in the Villa Albani showing the amorous Polyphemos sitting on a rock (plate 4).[8] In these examples, we find established types of scene and figure, fundamental paradigms of scenic and figural composition, which derive from different epochs of Greek art but which are used, side by side, in the different periods of Roman image-making. In Augustan, as in Flavian times, traditional types of both Classical and Hellenistic art were taken up and visually exploited.

The various periods of Roman art are thus not primarily or fundamentally differentiated from each other by the selection of specific, exemplary figure-types and narrative models from a particular period of Greek art at any one time. Rather, they bear the clear stamp of the Roman style current at the time, but in a quite different respect – that of technical execution. The 'Idolino' has the spare, dry physique of the early Empire; the Vatican youth the flabby, plumpish form of the Flavian era. In the same way, the relief of the She-wolf displays the sharp, precise chisel-work of the Augustan period, that of Polyphemos the loose sketchy methods of Flavian times. In effect, there are similar types of scenes executed in different styles, and a related temporal style encompassing figural types that belong to different formal traditions rooted in the history of Greek art.

The Roman language of imagery has its primary framework in its typological borrowings from the Greek past, just as written or spoken language has its frame in its syntax and vocabulary. By the term

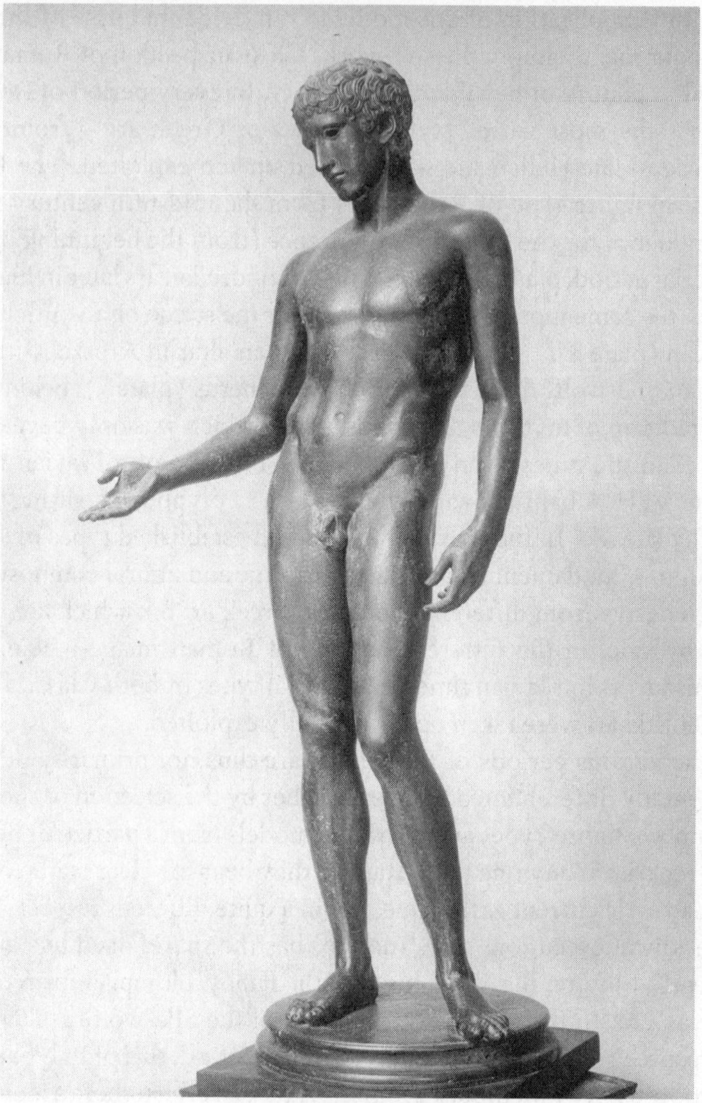

Plate 1: Statue of youth, so-called 'Idolino', beginning of Imperial period

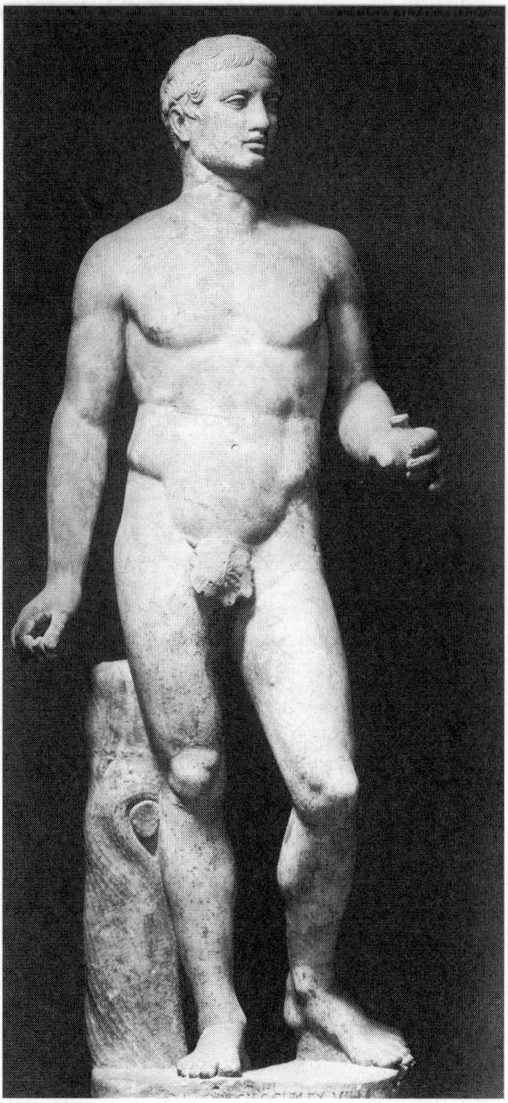

Plate 2: Statue of youth, Flavian period

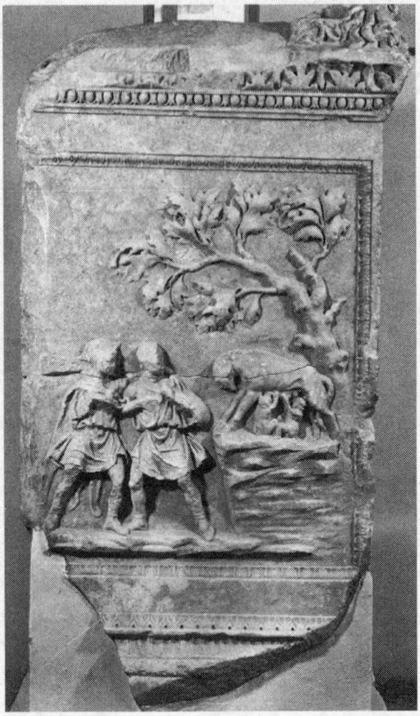

Plate 3: Altar depicting the Roman She-wolf, the Twins and the Shepherds, Augustan period

'typology', I mean here a broad range of schemas from basic patterns of representation (such as mythological landscape reliefs or the Polykleitian physique) to the more or less conscious use and reformulation of specific earlier models and the faithful copying of individual original pieces.[9] This range will be denoted in what follows by the expressions 'pattern of representation' or 'mode of representation', on the one hand, and by 'figural type' on the other. Temporal style, by contrast, can – for my present purposes – be classed as a secondary phenomenon, as it is for linguistic structure. In this context, I shall not deal with style but confine myself to the question of its relationship to the typological language of imagery which is my principal theme.

In the choice of models, the extent of pluralism is remarkable. The range was such that it cannot have been determined by a consensus of taste in artistic forms – not on the part of whole periods, nor of different

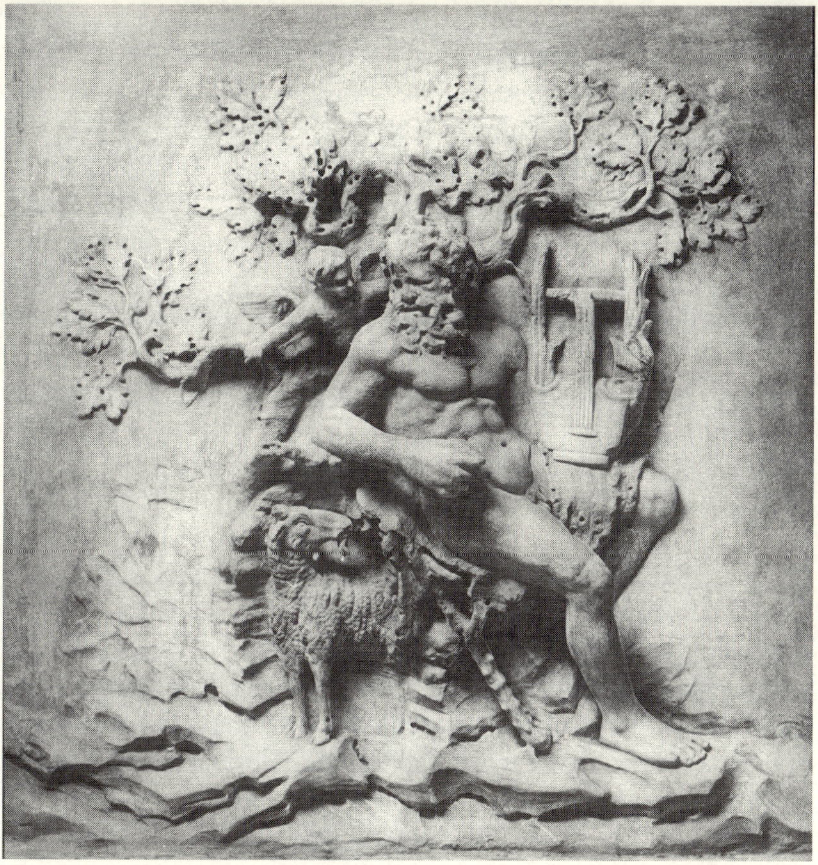

Plate 4: Relief with Polyphemos, Flavian period

social groups, nor even of single individuals, clients or artists. For, even within a single group of monuments – even on one and the same monument – we can find a diversity of heterogeneous models. Take the Ara Pacis, dedicated under Augustus in 9 BC. There, the great frieze with its Imperial procession (plates 28, 30) closely follows the Classical Parthenon frieze (plates 27, 29, 31).[10] The small frieze, however, with its sacrificial procession (plate 44), can hardly be seen as a reflection of Classical models.[11] Even more plainly, a relief with a battle-scene in Mantua (plate 16) – which must come from a public building in Rome of roughly similar (if slightly later) date – diverges radically from the clearly separated combat groups of Classical friezes, and espouses instead a crowded composition that follows Hellenistic models.[12] Two centuries later and a thousand miles away, we find the situation little changed. On the great monument of Lucius Verus from Ephesos, the scene representing the Imperial family (plate 5) still stands in the Classical tradition of the great frieze of the Ara Pacis. The battle-scene, however, belongs to the Hellenistic tradition of the Mantua relief.[13]

The case of the Aeneas panel on the Ara Pacis (plate 46) can help us refine this analysis further. The scene as a whole stands in the tradition of Hellenistic landscape. A fair comparison, for instance, is the depiction of a Dionysos sanctuary on the mid-second-century BC Telephos frieze from the Great Altar of Pergamon (plate 6).[14] The figure of Aeneas, however, resembles the draped figures of Greek High Classicism – for example, that of a grave-relief from Salamis (plate 7).[15] Again, the group of the second sacrificial assistant with the pig follows a Hellenistic model, as preserved for instance in paintings from Delos (plate 8).[16] Finally, the depiction of Aeneas himself – while generally Classical in type – is enriched by details developed only in later periods. Hence the sharply drawn folds around the legs appear in similar form on the late Hellenistic Poseidon of Melos.[17] The patterns of representation, figural types and formulae developed in Greek art are thus appropriated and exploited with breathtaking flexibility – sometimes for the whole composition, sometimes for single figures and groups, sometimes for yet smaller details.

Beside all this, there are the genuinely stylistic factors. The Augustan style of the relief binds the figures and objects closely on to a plane; frontal and profile views predominate; the figures are clearly outlined; everything joins in forming a clear and comprehensible composition. All this corresponds to the general effects of Greek High Classical relief.[18] Moreover, the actual technique of marble-carving combines a differentiated and subtle surface movement with a clear accentuation through planes and lines. Here, too, we may recognise a 'Classical taste' in a general sense. The style of the relief and the technique of marble-working apply to the panel as a whole, independently of the heterogeneous sources of each element within it. Here a temporally specific, Augustan, style is very clear – as it is also on the other reliefs

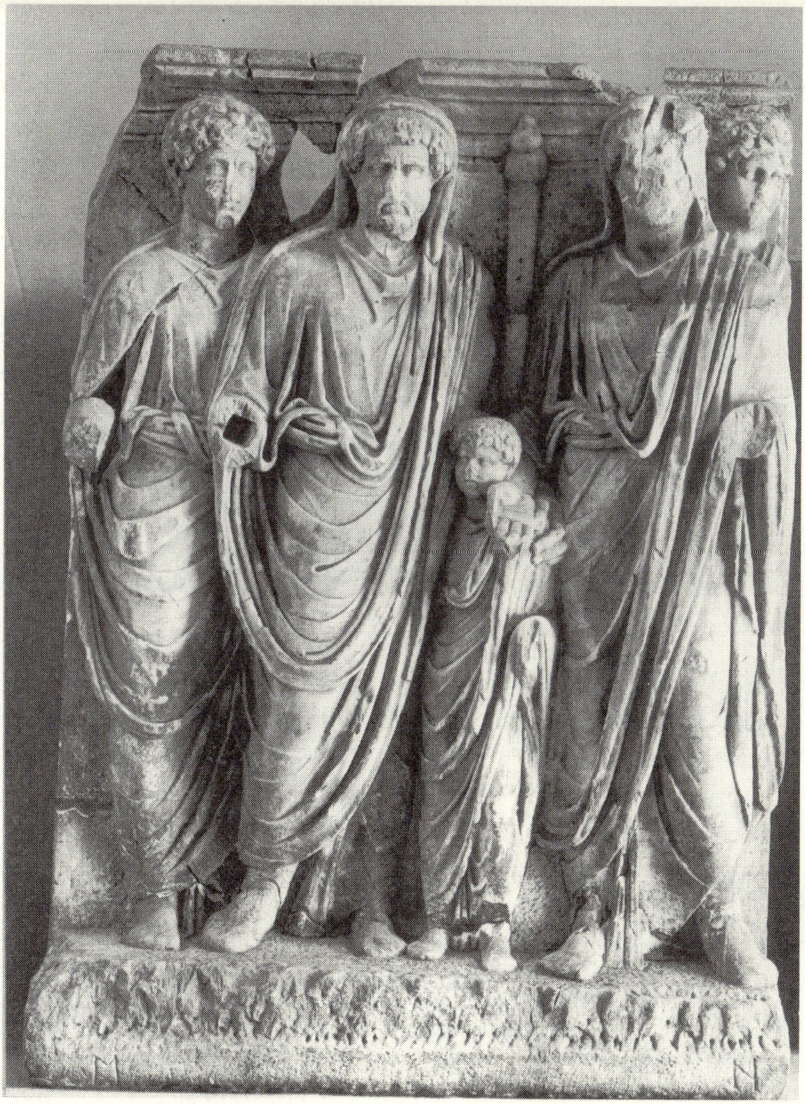

Plate 5: Scene from the monument of Lucius Verus at Ephesos depicting the adoption by Hadrian of Antoninus Pius, Marcus Aurelius and Lucius Verus

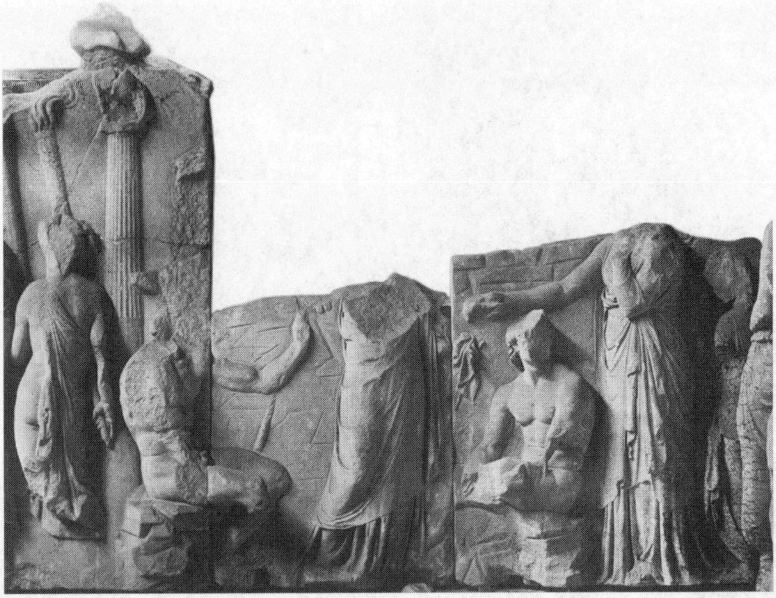

Plate 6: Telephos frieze, Altar of Pergamon

of the Ara Pacis. This style takes its lead in important respects from Classical models.

In principle, therefore, we must distinguish between – on the one hand – modes of representation, figural types and formulae for detail which may be traced back to different epochs in Greek art, and – on the other hand – a conception of relief, together with a specific craft technique, whereby the heterogeneous elements of the work are presented in a unified 'style'. According to the distinction I suggested above,[19] this 'style' is an aspect of the general – more or less consciously and programmatically chosen – pattern of representation; the figural types and formulae, however, belong to a collectively disposable cultural property, and the result of their use is a differentiated visual language.

Yet objections to the heterogeneous character of this visual language remain. For if the choice of models does not depend on the taste and style of different periods, social groups or individuals, then on what does it depend? Is it a learned form of game-playing? Is it a symptom of Roman culture's poverty of invention? A chaos of forms?

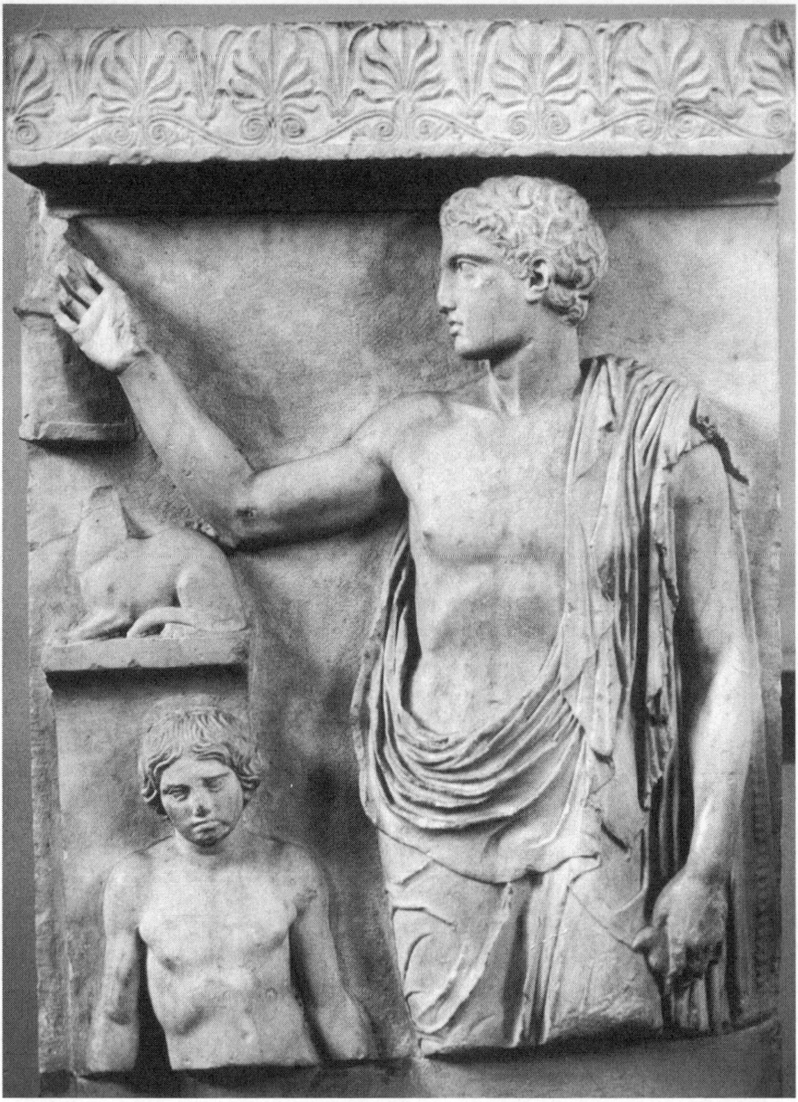

Plate 7: Grave stele from Salamis, 450–430/20 BC

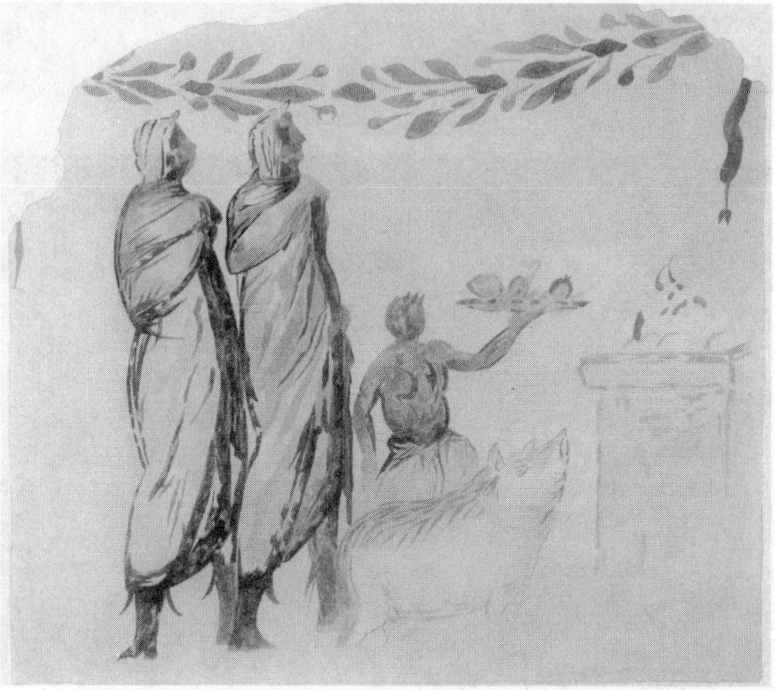

Plate 8: Painted altar, Delos, Hellenistic period

The works of art so far discussed point to a different solution. On the Lucius Verus monument from Ephesos, the dynastic relief depicting the Imperial family and the battle-scene stand in two quite different formal traditions. Yet those traditions had – from very early Imperial times – already been employed to determine the way the two kinds of subject-matter were represented. This prompts us to ask whether the use of the different formal – which is to say, 'typological' – traditions was dependent on content.[20] The question suggests itself above all for another reason: in historical actuality, when a commission was to be awarded to a particular sculptor or painter, as a rule it was undoubtedly the *content* of the work that proved the decisive factor, with the form only an issue of secondary consideration.[21]

As a provisional thesis, this amounts to the following: Roman art based its choice of visual paradigms not primarily on considerations of style or taste, but according to content and subject. It settled on different patterns, drawing on different periods of Greek art, for the different classes of subject-matter. This content-orientated approach was in principle dominant through all periods of Roman art, regardless of the style of the time.[22]

In my discussion, references to the use of 'Classical' and 'Hellenistic' patterns or models in late Hellenistic and Roman art should primarily be taken to apply, purely descriptively, to the employment of the various forms. By the terms 'Classical' and 'Hellenistic' I mean to state – following what has been established in contemporary research – that these forms had arisen in certain epochs of Greek art. But this does not necessarily imply that, when these forms were borrowed by Roman artists, there was a conscious recourse to this or that epoch of the past. Besides deliberate retrospection, there is undoubtedly also the possibility of the simple disposition of established forms, without reflection on their historical pedigree. This question remains to be taken up again in my conclusion.

NOTES

1. Zanker (1973) 44ff. Below, p. 47.
2. Wegner (1966) 9ff., pls. 1ff.
3. Brendel (1979) 105ff. It is strange that appeal has to be made to the very cursory remarks of Rodenwaldt (1931) for support for this widespread thesis. Compare Rodenwaldt (1935) 25ff., (1936), esp. 86.
4. The problematic nature of the transference to Roman art of the model of development devised for Greek art is often emphasised, especially by Brendel (1979) 99ff. and Settis (1982) 161ff.
5. Zanker (1974) 30ff., no. 28.
6. Helbig[4] I, no. 443 (W. Fuchs); Heintze (1962) 28, fig. 7; Zanker (1974), 39, no. 38.
7. Del Vita (1934) 429–33, pls. 15–16.
8. Schreiber (1894) pl. 65; *Brunn/Bruckmann* pl. 627a; Helbig[4] IV, no. 3302 (P. Zanker).
9. The range of possibilities and terms is given in Lippold (1923) 2ff. For criticism, see Zanker (1974) xvii. The Latin concepts of *interpretatio*, *imitatio* and *aemulatio* (Wünsche (1972)) cover this same spectrum, though with a one-sided orientation towards the creative process (see chapter 2, n.14). The concept of the *exemplum* (on which see Kornhardt (1936)) in my view takes us further: I thank C. Hibschmann for this reference. But I abstain from suggesting a new terminological system: the foundation for what follows is

the distinction between the phenomena of typology and of temporal style, which in a few cases may overlap, but are in principle different. Compare in general Schweitzer (1969), esp. 173ff., 176ff. The widest signification of what is here subsumed under 'type' corresponds to the concept of 'mode' in recent art history: compare n. 22 below.

10. Simon (1967), pls. 10ff. See below, pp. 49f.
11. Simon (1967), pl. 9, lower. See below, pp. 78f.
12. Koeppel (1983), esp. 81f., 129ff., no. 33. Below, pp. 39–41.
13. Eichler (1971), esp. 109ff., 127ff.; Oberleitner *et al.* (1978) 70f., 81ff.
14. *AvP* III 2 (1910), pl. 32.2.
15. Diepolder (1931), pl. 6.
16. Bulard (1926) pls. V 1, XI 1, XIII 1, XVIII 1, XIX, XXI, XXV 1; fig. 54.
17. Schäfer (1968).
18. Compare once again the grave-relief from Salamis (above, n.15). Here, structural differences between the Augustan and the Classical relief, especially in the relation between the figure and the background, cannot be overlooked; this is especially clear when viewing the heads from an angle (I thank I. Kress for this comment). But the effect achieved is similar.
19. p. 8 above.
20. There are forerunners in this approach. Especially important is Blanckenhagen (1942) 310ff. A particular problem in that essay is the concept of 'genre-style': first, because his concept of the 'genre' is not clearly defined and does not correspond to the phenomenon of the diverse methods of representation; secondly, because his concept of 'style' obscures the fundamental difference between this phenomenon and that of temporal style. Equally contrived is the idea that temporal style originates through the dominance of a 'genre-style' within the general production of works of art of its period. Finally, the classification of all 'genre-styles' into a polar spectrum extending from court art to popular art is difficult to uphold, and presumably devised mainly so as to be compatible with the polar opposition of state and individual. Much more flexible is Brendel (1979) 133ff.
21. On the strongly content-based orientation of Roman concepts of art in general: Jucker (1950) 18ff. Typical are Cicero's views on the fitting out of his villa near Tusculum: Becatti (1951) 90ff.
22. For recent studies which imply the semantic structure here expounded, see Zanker in *Classicisme*, 299ff. and (1983), esp. 27ff.; Hölscher (1980a) 317ff. and (1982), esp. 215; Schröder (1989); Cain (1985) 146ff. For post-antique art history, similar viewpoints have long since played a part in the theory of 'modes': see especially Bialostocky (1982) 12–42, esp. 14 with reference to Meyer Schapiro (1944), esp. 181, Gombrich (1953) (on Poussin). I thank S. Lehmann for directing me to these works.

CHAPTER 4

Battle-scenes: the tradition of Hellenistic pathos

Roman battle-scenes, almost without exception, stand in a tradition which must have undergone a variety of manifestations in Hellenistic art. The first stage can be clearly recognised in the Alexander Mosaic from Pompeii (late second century BC) (plate 9), an excellent copy of an important painting dating from the late fourth century BC soon after the death of Alexander the Great.[1] The whole composition of this picture is characterised by the new concept of space of early Hellenistic times.

Battle-scenes of the Classical period, whether mythical or contemporary in their subject-matter, whether in large-scale painting or on vases, had broken up the event into single combats.[2] Each figure is related exclusively to its immediate opponent. The individual combat-groups, however, do not stand in a realistic relationship to each other: if warriors on the same side face in different directions and have opponents both in front of and behind them, this cannot be interpreted as an overall tactical situation. Each combat-group is arranged on its own; the spatial relations between the figures are meant to be 'real' only in so far as they comply with the direct actions of the figures.[3] This gives expression to that immediacy of human interaction which characterises the idea of individual and action in the earlier Greek epochs.

In the painting, on the other hand, there is a multiple interrelation of actions within a coherent surrounding space. Alexander and the Macedonians attack from the left, press on the Persians in the centre, a detachment of cavalry with spears at the slope encircles the Persians from behind and wheels to the right round a standard, the Great King's charioteer drives the horses towards the right foreground in flight.[4] Each figure has its place and its rôle within this overall spatial

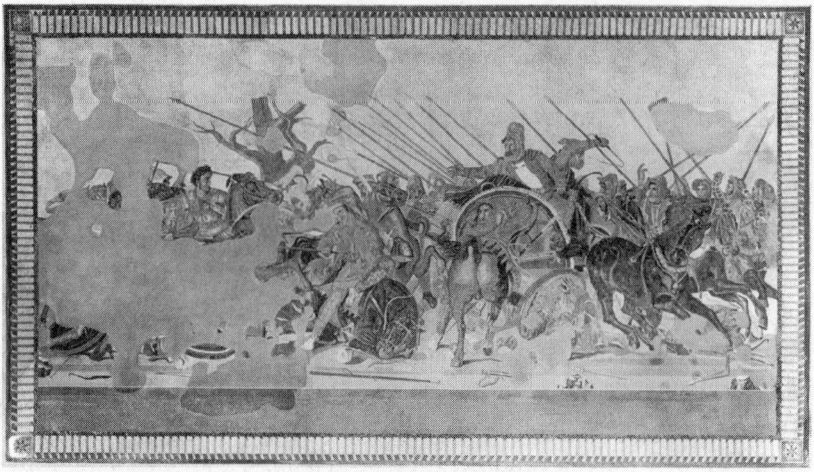

Plate 9

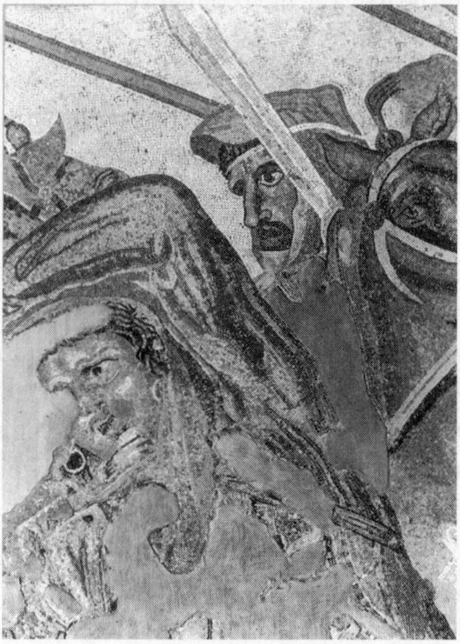

Plate 10

Plates 9–13: The Alexander Mosaic, copy of the late second century BC of a painting of the late fourth century BC, from the House of the Faun in Pompeii

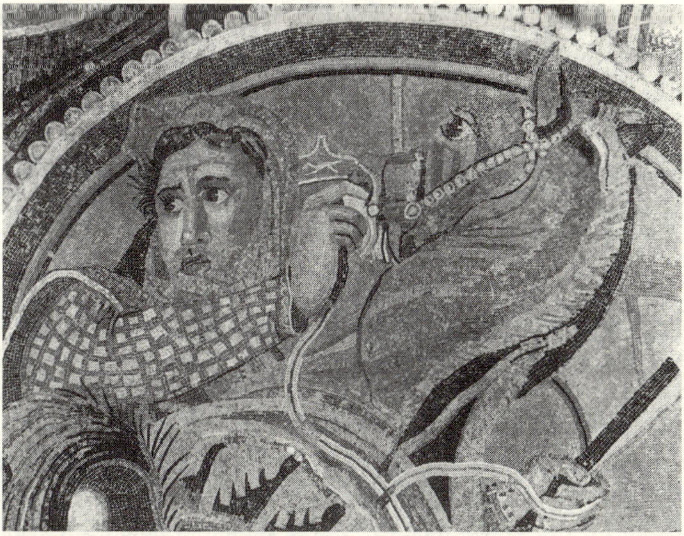

Plate 11

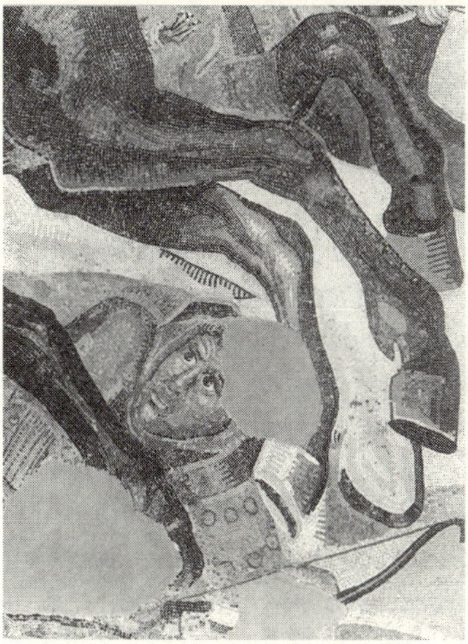

Plate 12

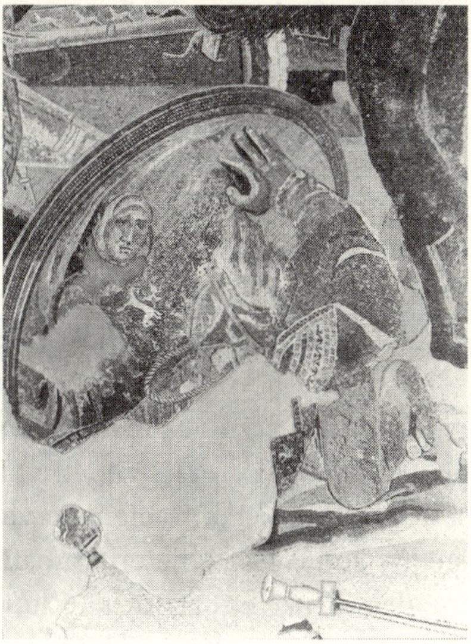

Plate 13

composition. A consequence of this conception is that the forms are pushed together into masses, and thus can join together in collective movements. The individual is understood through his relationship to the all-embracing coherence of the action.[5] It could be argued that here is a symptom of the conditions of the times, which harnessed the individual to collective contexts, stretching beyond his personal radius of action.

One of the most arresting aspects of the painting is the way in which so many individual destinies are contained in it: a prominent Persian, who has thrown himself at the last minute into the path of the charging Alexander; another, who with extreme difficulty holds a shying horse ready for his king to escape; a third, whose horse collides with the turning chariot; three fallen Persians besides, who are being run down by the chariot, one under the hooves of the horses, two others threatened by the huge, heavily nailed wheel, against which one of them tries to brace his shield. Again, in the midst of the Macedonians, a Persian who is being overtaken and cut down; and in the bottom left-hand corner the apparent remnants of a Macedonian who has paid for victory with his life and, in an agonised posture, falls headlong. Nowhere are the victors and the defeated united in the same context of action and fate as in Classical battle-scenes.[6] In the mosaic, certainly, this isolation of individual fate does not conflict with the coherence of the overall context. On the contrary, the rôle of the individual in the overriding whole can only have become a pictorial subject for the sake of depicting just such isolation. The new conception of space is a precondition for this isolation of personal destiny.

Here it is significant that it is the defeated, above all, who are portrayed with great sympathy. The range is wide: from the heroic self-sacrifice of the nobleman who hurls himself into the path of his enemy and is immediately threatened by three spear-points, through the despairing efforts of the 'horse-tamer' to the gruesome fates of those who are caught under the hooves and wheels of the royal chariot.

All this is presented with a pathos which was hitherto unthinkable. The pain-distorted countenance of the man transfixed in between the two kings (plate 10) is as effectively framed by his upraised arm as is the tense face of the 'horse-tamer' by the chariot-wheel (plate 11);

of the fallen man under the chariot, only the terrified glance from under the deadly whirl of dark horses' shanks is shown (plate 12); and the other fallen man's despairing expression is heightened, to the greatest effect, as a mask-like mirror-image reflected in his shield (plate 13). Just how consciously this moment of pathos is contrived is shown by the Persians behind the chariot with their pitiful gestures, as if displaying, as onlookers within the picture, the emotion that the viewer of the picture should feel.

For all that, sharply contrasting effects are sought after: the wide-eyed Alexander, charging in a straight line, as against the bent, tortured Persian noble; the latter's powerful fending-off movement, against the collapse of his horse as it bleeds to death; Alexander's well-aimed dynamism against the vague, powerless gesture of the Great King, and in turn against the bitter resolution of the whip-cracking charioteer; the frenzied energy of the shying horse against the helpless paralysis of the Persians behind.

The Alexander painting, in its depiction of fate and pathos, collectivity and isolation, power and destruction, is a uniquely bold leap forward into the new political, social and psychological universe of the Hellenistic. Such a manifestation could probably be achieved at that time only in painting: only in certain aspects did the other genres follow suit.

The battle on the 'Alexander Sarcophagus' from the Royal Necropolis at Sidon (late fourth century BC), which seems to be dependent on the painting, dissolves the coherent action into individual groups made up of entirely conventional types.[7] By comparison with Classical battle-friezes, however, the events are so densely packed together that the impression emerges, as on the mosaic, of an indissoluble crowd scene.

More significant is the great victory monument of Attalos I of Pergamon (*ca.* 220 BC), which portrayed a number of defeated enemies, Celts and Persians, on an elongated base (plate 14).[8] The victors were not included in the representation. They were implied by the location in which the monument stood: the sacred precinct of Athena, the bestower of victory. And they were put into concrete form by the person of King Attalos himself, whose equestrian statue was mounted

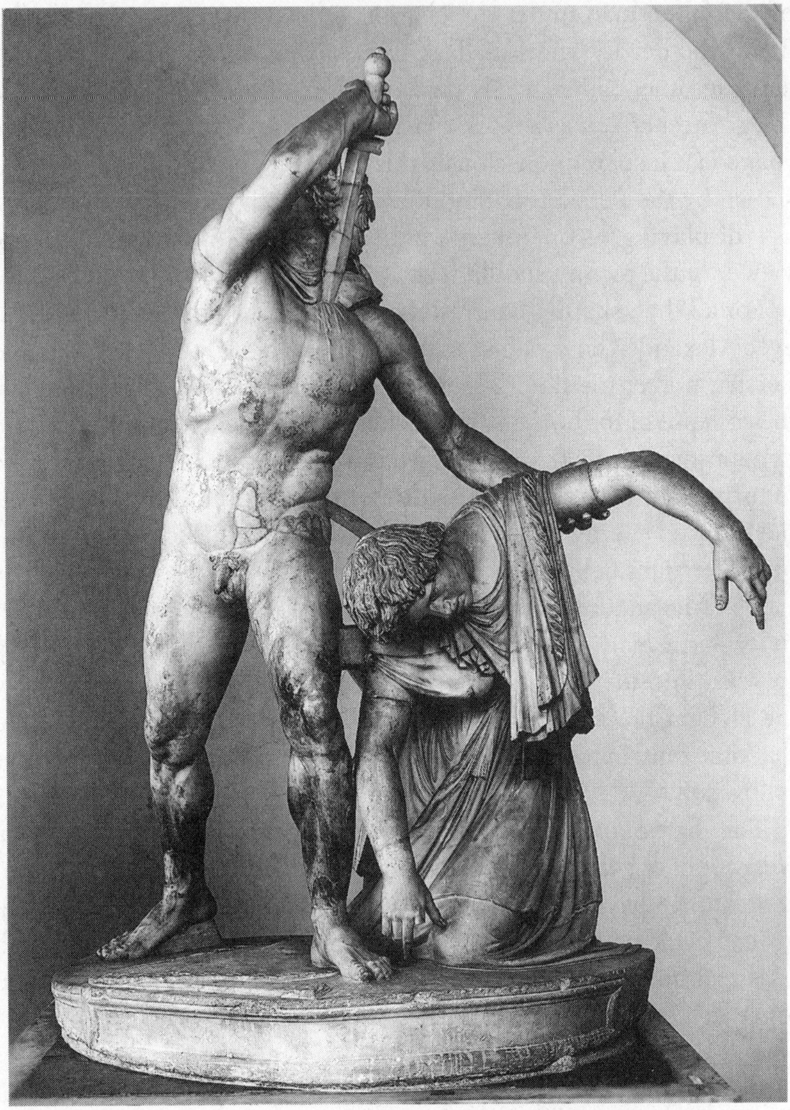

Plate 14: Group of the 'Ludovisi Gaul', Roman copy of Greek original

on a separate base, but doubtless formed the point of reference for the statues of the defeated. The complete separation of victors and enemies, especially the portrayal of the conquered in isolated groups, followed the logic of the concept shaped by the Alexander painting. Here too, furthermore, individual destinies are recorded in many different facets: a Persian dying quietly by himself; a broken, collapsing Celt with his now useless trumpet; above all, the Celtic chieftain who, faced with the pursuing enemy, has stabbed his wife and is now taking his own life. This group too is stamped with high pathos: killing one's own wife, especially when done out of pity, and suicide in hopeless circumstances, are motifs of the greatest emotional power. And this effect too is achieved with sharp contrasts of form: below, the woman slumping forwards in collapse with her heavy masses of drapery and her dying face turned away; above, the figure of the naked man, stretching powerfully upwards, culminating in his exotic physiognomy, the main vehicle of expression, which is effectively distanced from the body, in profile view, by the arm.

The multiple-figure memorial of Attalos II on the Athenian Acropolis (*ca.* 160 BC) goes further still.[9] Here were portrayed the celebrated struggles to defend Hellenism against mythical and historical barbarian foes – once again, evidently, only in the form of the defeated enemies: giants, Amazons, Persians and Celts. It must have been an immense accumulation of desperation in self-defence, resignation in collapse and limpness in death, made effective by the weight of the diffused misery. Here too the historical victors to whom these mythical and historical figures relate, Attalos II and Eumenes II, seem to have been present in the form of separately erected figures; and these not even taking the form of equestrian statues, which would have linked them to the subject of the fighting, but as colossi standing beside it, with attributes of deification – thus rising, in every way, above the surrounding scene.

The monument of Aemilius Paullus in Delphi (after 168 BC) (plate 15)[10] shows how widespread such attitudes were. Here the frieze at the top of the pillar contained not isolated combatants but, in a somewhat traditional composition, the fighting between the Romans and the Greeks at Pydna; but the victorious commander is not shown.

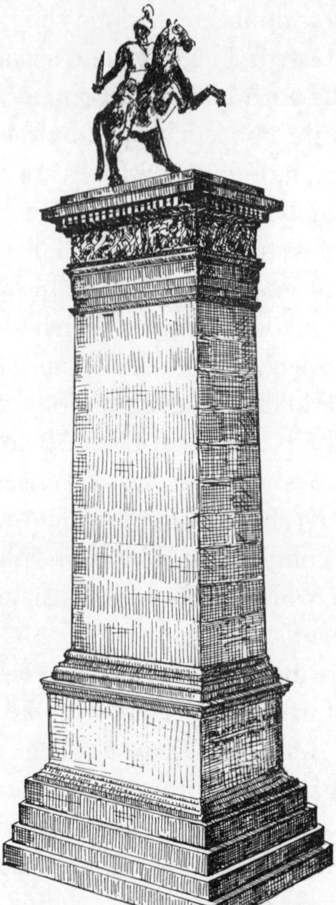

Plate 15: Monument of Aemilius Paullus, Delphi

The rider-figure who bursts into the relief ground on the frontal side, sharply foreshortened, cannot possibly be Aemilius Paullus.[11] It is not only the back view – extremely inauspicious for the leading figure – which speaks against the identification, but above all the fact that his opponent carries a Roman oblong shield: the rider is therefore a Greek. Aemilius Paullus, in contrast, was raised above the anonymous events of the frieze in the form of a bronze equestrian statue. Not only the conquered enemies, but the Roman troops too constitute, literally and metaphorically, the substructure for the fame of the single, great commander.

The conception of such battle scenes has its counterpart in the dramatised, 'tragic' historiography of Hellenistic times.[12] It was the goal of this school of historians to give one the feeling of experiencing their history. They wanted to bring the events home to the reader in a lively, credible way, to awaken pathos, to arouse horror and anger, fear and pity. Human beings take the centre stage, mostly on their own, acting and suffering, entrusted to the power of Fortune. The main exponents are Duris of Samos and Phylarchos (early third century BC). Both of them were later casualties of a verdict inspired by Classicism;[13] as a result, they largely dropped out of the tradition and are now recoverable only indirectly, Duris especially in Diodoros' extracts on Agathokles,[14] Phylarchos in Plutarch's *Lives* of Agis and of Kleomenes.[15] Tendencies in this direction can be found from the fourth century BC onwards, antecedents even earlier. At that time they may have obtained specific reinforcement from the fact that the Aristotelian principles of tragedy were carried over into historiography.[16] At all events Hellenistic battle-scenes, in their essentials as well as in their formal methods, find endorsement both in Aristotle and in the representatives of 'tragic' historiography.[17]

Already in Aristotle, the most important means of generating pathos is 'action leading to destruction or great pain, such as deaths on the open stage, excessive sufferings, woundings and the like'.[18] Duris and Phylarchos portrayed such scenes in very explicit form: Duris especially must have presented this kind of thing in fullest detail (*kata meros*). The panorama of gruesome fates on the Alexander Mosaic is designed for just the same effect. Pathos is enhanced still further if, in the chaos of defeat, the losers are done to death by their own comrades;[19] in this motif, too, 'tragic' historiography matches the mosaic.[20]

Yet, for the arousal of fear and pity (*phobos* and *eleos*) over and above the general suffering, Aristotle especially recommends the murder, under duress, of relations and friends.[21] This point too was taken up by 'tragic' historiography; with it belongs suicide, even though this is not mentioned by Aristotle.[22] Phylarchos presented, with great persuasive power and to dramatic effect, the end of Kleomenes and his comrades, who in desperate straits kill either themselves or each other.[23] Later, too, the climaxes in 'tragic' historiography continue to take the form of the suicide of the persecuted and mutual killing of relations and friends.[24] In exactly this spirit, the group of the 'Ludovisi Gaul' (*ca.* 220 BC) presents the maximum heightening of accumulated misery on the part of defeated enemies.

The feeling for such extreme situations is only one aspect of the general eye for the deeds and destinies of the individual at this period.[25] Just as in tragedy only a few heroic figures are given prominence, so too 'tragic' historiography centred the diverse events of each successive epoch around individual figures – a clear example is Duris' portrayal of Agathokles.[26] Likewise, in the Alexander Mosaic the multi-figured surge of battle culminates in the confrontation of the two kings.

Aristotle and the historiographers alike turn their gaze on the suffering and the defeated.[27] The 'tragic' historiographers took up, in an entirely new way, an interest in all those who fell under the wheels of fate and history. This angle of vision is very clear in the mosaic, and the perspective is made absolute in the Celtic memorials of Pergamon. Both the self-sacrifice of the Persian nobles for their king and the actions of the Celts show that the defeated, though unmistakably presented as enemies, are emphatically not judged in a one-sided, negative way.

To achieve such effects, the literary genres had to strive especially for vividness. In fact the demand for graphic clarity (*enargeia*), the intention to bring the events before one's very eyes (*pro ommatōn tithenai*), was already established for tragedy by Aristotle, and was promoted by 'tragic' historiography – with the same formulations – to become the central goal.[28] Events from the immediately preceding past were regarded as especially effective, and vividness enhanced by describing factual details and pointed sub-plots in as rich a way as possible.[29]

To convey material reality, pictorial art had no obstacles to surmount. Even so, the idea of *enargeia* became important for Hellenistic visual art too, and specifically in the context of battle-paintings.[30] In the Alexander Mosaic and other historical scenes, admittedly, the choice of historical event derives not from artistic considerations, but from political imperatives. Yet it is significant that this very painting, with its highly topical subject, is probably the most realistically detailed work in the whole of Greek art. Through the minutely accurate reproduction of clothing, equipment, armour and jewellery, Greek and Oriental alike, the episode is brought home to the viewer with unnatural clarity.[31] Beyond this, there are touches of tremendous realism which fulfil the dramatic effect: Alexander's lost helmet, which heightens the exposure and peril of the victor; the broken spear-tip piercing the chest of the fallen horse, along which the blood flows on to the ground, to run as a thin trickle ending in the puddle under its mouth; the swollen veins on the hind-quarters of the shying horse and on the heads of the chariot-horses, which bring out the explosive panic of the situation. Likewise the merciless realism with which Alexander runs through the Persian noble, followed up by two other lances; or the chariot-wheel, with an almost audible grinding, crushes the shield on to the fallen Persian; or the horses trample the other fallen men – this too is one of the means whereby *enargeia* is achieved.[32]

How are such resemblances between historiography and the visual arts to be understood? When we enquire about the purposes of the two genres, differences are also to be seen: the battle-scenes are state monuments, their celebration is entirely from the victor's viewpoint; historiography on the other hand normally preserves an attitude of detachment.[33] One might well wonder whether the principles of such historiography may be sensibly applied to the interpretation of political monuments, with their quite different perspectives and intended effects; in particular, whether the concern with the fate of the defeated, which is expressly present in historiography, is really a credible theme for state art, or whether the victory monuments should be understood in a different way.[34] One might rather expect to find parallels for the works of figural art in the ruler panegyrics.[35]

It is evident, however, that the dramatic and 'tragic' style of representation is more or less independent of the communicative purposes of the different genres. Related phenomena occur across a wide range of Hellenistic culture. There were similar tendencies in historical epic.[36] And mythical subjects were often similarly treated in the visual arts: Niobe and her children, Laokoön and his sons, the ill-treated Marsyas, the companions of Odysseus – all undergo, with high pathos, their downfall through a terrible fate which in some cases overtakes them in an impersonal way.[37] 'Tragic' historiography is undoubtedly just one manifestation of the more general tendencies of the Hellenistic age, in the specific area of historical narrative. Statecraft and historiography, therefore, need not necessarily have developed in conscious linkage with each other. The phenomena expounded here are types of interpretation and techniques of representation that could be used for different genres, functions and subjects.[38]

But beyond this, it is clear that the principles of 'tragic' historiography could be enlisted also in the services of more glorificatory art. It is true that we know too little of Hellenistic ruler panegyric to discern how far it took up the 'tragic' or dramatic technique of portrayal.[39] But even 'tragic' historiography had, in its tendency to compose each epoch around the figure of one protagonist,[40] a trait which complied well with the purpose of glorification: if this figure was a hero judged positively, like Agis or Kleomenes, then this offered a perspective that was really quite close to that of the glorificatory monuments.[41] In fact Cicero, in his 56 BC letter to Lucceius, expressed the wish for the commemoration of his consulate in the literary terms of 'tragic' historiography, thus glossing over the boundary between historiography and encomium.[42]

In the Celtic monuments of Pergamon, too, the involvement in the grief of the defeated means no diminution of the glory of the victor: his position remains unaffected. On the contrary, he is elevated so far above the conquered enemy that their misfortunes unfold in a separate field of their own. As a counter-world of woe, the defeated side can awake the pity of the viewer and thereby heighten the glory of the victor.

'Tragic' historiography and political monuments have admittedly different functions and intended effects, and they may have developed without any altogether direct mutual influence. Yet, in their drive for emotionally effective impetus, and in the motifs and formal means employed to that end, they are similar.

NOTES

1. Fuhrmann (1931); Rumpf (1962); Hölscher (1973) 122ff.; Giuliani (1977); Andreae (1977); Schefold (1979) 9ff.; Nylander (1983) 19ff. and (1982).

2. In large-scale painting, especially the mural of the Battle of Marathon in the Stoa Poikile: Robert (1895); Hölscher (1973) 50ff. Among mythological subjects, Amazon battles are especially informative: Bothmer (1957) *passim*. A good example is the lekythos by Aison in Naples: Simon and Hirmer (1976) pl. 220.
3. On this see Hölscher (1973) 28ff., 78ff.
4. For a different interpretation of the action, see Nylander (1983). In general, the essentials do not depend on the objective explanation of the picture given here; this hypothesis merely gives them an extra pointedness.
5. Hölscher (1973) 162ff.
6. On this, see Fehr (1977) 189f.
7. Graeve (1970) pls. 24ff.
8. Schober (1936) and (1951) 53ff.; Künzl (1971); Wenning (1978); Coarelli (1978); Özgan (1981); Hölscher (1985a); Schalles (1985) 68ff. The work of Schalles was already known to me at the time of the preparation of my essay in manuscript. I thought that I owed it to the author not to deal with it, so as not to have to burden it, before its appearance, with polemic against his rejection of one of my theses (below, n. 34). In so far as his conclusions agree with mine, they were reached independently.
9. Schober (1951) 121ff.; Palma (1981); Hölscher (1985a) 123ff. A parallel for a vanquished figure in defensive posture, without a victorious opponent, is the Gaul from Delos who, because of his forward movement and the absence of any trace on the plinth, cannot have had an enemy either over him or immediately beside him; see most recently Marcadé (1969) 119ff., 363ff., pl. 80; Coarelli (1982), esp. 129.
10. Kähler (1965).
11. So Kähler (1965) 17f. The counter-proposal of Bonanno (1976) 5f. fails because the rider in question is located on a subordinate face of the pillar, right at the back.
12. On the 'tragic' school of historiography, see especially Schwartz (1897) 560ff.; Wehrli (1947); Fritz (1958); Zegers (1959); Strasburger (1966) 78ff.; Flach (1973) 14ff. On the wider significance of this historiography, see Strasburger (1966), Meier (1970) 211ff. The reflections in what follows were already intimated in Hölscher (1980b), esp. 354f.; (1985a) 130. Against them, Schalles (1985) 85ff. On this, see n.34 below.
13. See pp. 47f. below.
14. Diod. Sic. 19–21. See Schwartz, *RE* v 1 663–704, esp. 687f., s.v. Diodorus; v 2, 1853–6, esp. 1855, s.v. Duris.
15. On this see Kroymann, *RE Suppl.* 8, 471–89, s.v. Phylarchos.
16. Isokrates, from whom early 'tragic' historiography aggressively distances itself, opposes the description of battle tumults, cries of woe and shouts

of encouragement in the writing of history (*Paneg.* 97; similarly, *Euag.* 31): such things must therefore have been known already in his day, and been openly at the disposal of 'tragic' historiography as a starting-point. Ephoros, too, opposed a manner of representation which placed too much in the foreground 'the terrible and the wondrous' (*to deinon kai to thaumaston*; Strabo 7.3.9); 'the wondrous' (*to deinon*) then became an important term in 'tragic' historiography: Arist., *Poet.* 1453 b; Polyb. 2.56.7f.; Diod. Sic. 19.8.3f. In this connection, W. Schuller points me to Thucydides as well, and to his assessment by Connor (1984), summed up at 232f.

17. An important insight is that of Flashar (1984) that it is above all the 'pathetic' tragedy of the fourth century BC that underlies Aristotle's *Poetics*. It has often been assumed that the carrying-over of tragedy into historiography was implemented in Theophrastos' text *On History* (*Peri historiās*): see most fully Zegers (1959) 76ff. The problem can be set aside here.
18. Arist., *Poet.* 1452 b 11ff.; Zegers (1959) 14ff. With it goes the emphasis on suffering bravely borne: Zegers (1959) 19.
19. Already in the painting of the Battle of Marathon in the Stoa Poikile (*ca.* 460 BC), the Persians were shown pushing each other into the marsh in their flight: Paus. 1.15.3. Hölscher (1973) 53f., 67.
20. Diod. Sic. (Phylarchos) 20.12.1 and 7; 20.29.10. In addition, the structure of *peripeteia*, of equally great importance for Aristotle's theory of tragedy as it was for 'tragic' historiography (Zegers (1959) 47ff., cf. 19ff.), is characteristic of the Alexander Mosaic. Here, however, it is definitely suggested by the subject and therefore by the commission, and need not therefore have a purely artistic justification.
21. Arist., *Poet.* 1453 b 19ff.: cf. Zegers (1959) 11ff.
22. Compare Diod. Sic. 20.34.
23. Plut., *Cleom.* 27; cf. 31.
24. Livy 1.58.6ff.; Tac., *Hist.* 2.46ff.
25. Compare Latte (1958) 129f.
26. Zegers (1959) 43ff.; 75.
27. Explicitly in Polyb. 2.56.7–8; Strasburger (1966) 88; Meier (1970) 211ff.
28. Arist., *Poet.* 1455 a 22ff.; 1462 a 17; Polyb. 2.56.8; Zegers (1959) 15ff.; Flach (1973) 17ff.
29. Temporal closeness in 'tragic' historiography: Zegers (1959) 16f. Compare Arist., *Rh.* 1386 a 29ff.; 1386 b 1.
30. See p. 38 below.
31. Likewise in 'tragic' historiography: Zegers (1959) 17f.
32. With the same objective, 'tragic' historiography presented individual scenes which were entirely incidental to the course of history: Polyb. 2.56.10; Zegers (1959) 52f.

33. This fundamental difference of perspective led, for example, to Fortune playing a much greater rôle as a triggering factor in historiography (Zegers (1959) 27ff.) than in the public monuments.
34. It is essentially to these differences that Schalles (1985) attaches most weight, as against the connections that I had previously indicated (above, n. 8) between political monuments and 'tragic' historiography. But I never intended this association to be as close as Schalles takes it to be. The reflections worked out here seem to show that in many respects our standpoints are not so far apart – it is merely that he judges from the angle of political intent, I primarily from that of the visual language.
35. On the difference between historiography and encomium, see Lucian, *De hist.cons.* 7; Avenarius (1956) 13ff.
36. Ziegler (1966) 74ff., Latte (1958) 132.
37. Hölscher (1985a) 130ff. The importance of the part here played by general experience of the Hellenistic age is stressed by Latte (1958) 129. Compare Flach (1973) 21.
38. At any rate, the comparison between historiography and the visual arts, specifically from the point of view of liveliness of description, was a favourite theme: Plut., *De glor.Ath.* 347a, c; Polyb. 12.25h.2–4; cf. Dion. Hal., *Ant.Rom.* 11.1.3. Avenarius (1956) 139f. suspects that it originates from the theory of 'tragic' historiography. And certainly the correspondence between 'tragic' historiography and painting in the style of the Alexander Mosaic extends very widely: both were reproached, in the classicising view of art, for the insufficient care that they gave to stylistic aspects.
39. For a summary of the passages in Hellenistic ruler panegyric, I am indebted to M. Strauss.
40. See above, n.26.
41. In accord with the Aristotelian theory of tragedy, 'tragic' historiography took pains to portray the protagonists in as positive a light as possible: Zegers (1959) 20ff.
42. Cic., *Fam.* 5.12; Zegers (1959) 80ff.; Flach (1973) 30ff. Compare too Latte (1958) 132.

CHAPTER 5

Battle-scenes: their reception in Rome

In this spirit, the tradition of Hellenistic battle-representations was taken up in Rome. An important rôle must have been played by the Republican panel-paintings, known to us only from the written sources, which were carried round in triumphal processions and then exhibited in public spaces and buildings.[1] In them had been depicted, with a wealth of geographical information and topographic detail, the victorious campaigns. It can no longer be assumed today that this was a typically Roman form of representation;[2] its Hellenistic origin is at once proclaimed by the only name in this tradition recorded for Rome, that of the topographic painter Demetrios.[3] In the same way, according to Polybios, these paintings, together with other exhibits in the triumphal procession, were to promote that *enargeia*[4] which had been centrally important for the writing of Hellenistic history. This should primarily mean, for the third and second centuries, a similar level of detail in the portrayal of events and localities as the historians applied in their description of landscape and topography as an illustrative device.[5] In the last century of the Republic, on the other hand, more and more stirring and sensational effects were sought after, which fully corresponded to the pathetic tendencies of 'tragic' historiography.[6] Just as, in the triumphal procession of Pompey in 61 BC, a night-attack was portrayed in paintings, with the keeping of silence as part of it[7] – however we are to imagine this – so the representation of nocturnal events, with the suggestion of noise or lack of it, was a most effective part of the stock-in-trade of 'tragic' historiography in its pursuit of persuasive effects.[8] A similar quality attached to the pictures at Pompey's triumph showing the death of Mithridates, attended by the wives who shared his end, and of the sons

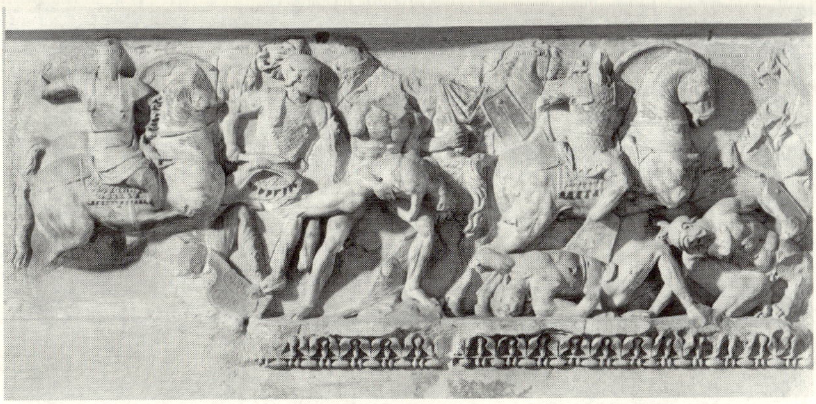

Plate 16: Battle-frieze, *ca.* mid-first century AD

and daughters previously put to death.[9] And at Caesar's triumph in 45 BC, the circumstances of his enemies' deaths were represented – the suicides of Lucius Scipio, Petreius and Cato.[10] Appian reports that the crowd broke out groaning at the sight of these pictures; his description of their subjects as 'sufferings' (*pathēmata*) once more reflects the Hellenistic source of this kind of art.

There are a number of monuments which prove that this tradition was continued into Imperial times. Immediately after Actium, it is true, the Temple of Apollo *in Circo* (*ca.* 20 BC) was decorated with a frieze in which single combats are lined up next to each other in the Classical manner.[11] But a relief in Palestrina of the same period, and the Mantua frieze of not much later (*ca.* mid-first century AD) (plate 16), take up once again the dense concentrations and strong gradations of depth of Hellenistic battle-scenes.[12] Roman ideology achieved hereby a greater emphasis on the superiority of the victors, shown in an upper register, leaping over the enemy who lie on the ground. The tormented postures of the latter carry on from the Hellenistic portrayals of death. On the Mantua frieze, the pathetic motif of the barbarian who, hard-pressed by his enemies, carries from the tumult of battle a dead comrade with all the beauty of youth, embodies all the features of 'tragic' historiography. Here again, glorification of one's own victory is not incompatible with sympathy for the fate of one's enemy, and even the

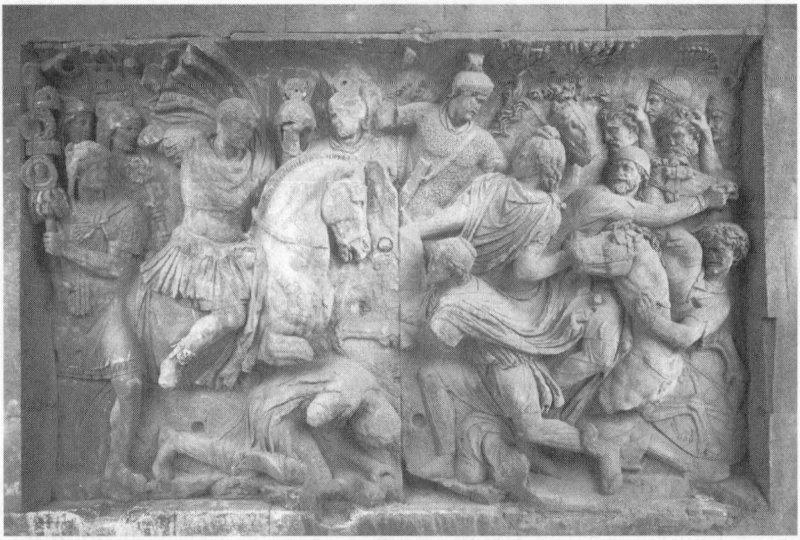

Plate 17

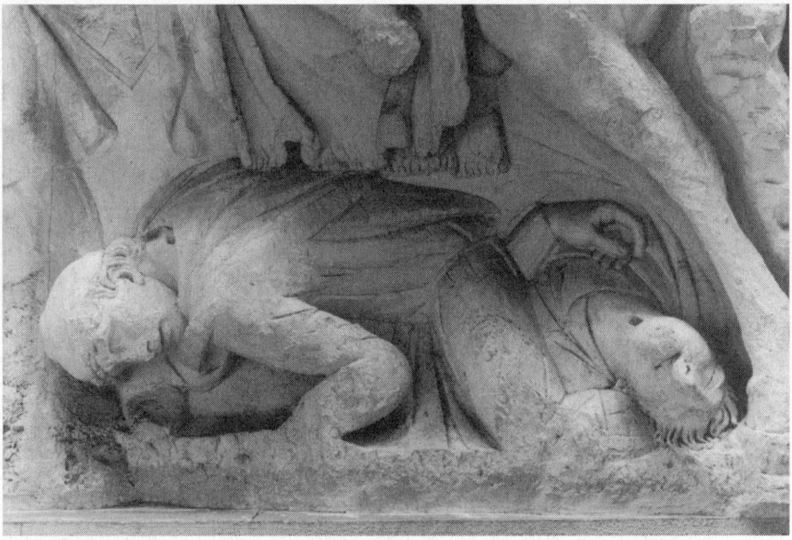

Plate 18

Plates 17–18: Trajanic battle-frieze, Arch of Constantine, Rome

recognition of some of his impressive traits. Conqueror and conquered are so far separated from each other that each can, to a great extent, be portrayed in his own glory or misery.

Even the total segregation of the victor from the defeated, as conceived in some of the Hellenistic monuments, found successors in the Roman period: on the 'Gemma Augustea' (AD 10–14), the pictorial concept of the ruler, triumphantly enthroned above a scene of subjugation, is elevated even by comparison with the monument of Aemilius Paullus;[13] while on the 'Grand Camée' (second quarter of the first century AD) the separation is made complete, as previously on the Pergamene Celtic monuments.[14] Where the defeated are no longer in direct, threatening confrontation with the victor, a space is created for the emotions, within which sympathy and pity can develop. The pitiful sufferings of the enemy only enhance the greatness of the Emperor.

The great Trajanic battle-frieze, which was reused on the Arch of Constantine (AD 312–15), stands directly in the Hellenistic tradition (plate 17).[15] The central scene with the Emperor is directly dependent on the composition of the Alexander painting. Here again the Roman version makes absolute the superiority of the victor: Trajan sweeps the enemy in front of him *en masse*; no opposing commander appears as an adversary. Yet, once more, motifs of the highest pathos are inserted: the severed Dacian heads, brandished at the Emperor by his own soldiers, scarcely distinguishable beside the faces of the still fleeing enemy; or the well-known figure of a dead man draped in the path of a horse as it bursts forward (plate 18).[16]

Trajan's Column (AD 106–13) contains not only numerous battle-compositions in the Hellenistic manner, but also other scenes of great 'tragic' effect: as where, in a beleaguered town, the Dacians in their droves seek death by poison administered from a large vessel by one of their leaders; the men push their way forward with outstretched arms, while others are already collapsing, held up and lamented over by their comrades, yet others lie lifeless on the ground, and a further part of the garrison seeks safety in flight (plate 19);[17] or where Decebalus, overtaken in a lonely forest after his long flight, eludes capture by his suicide (plate 20) and his sons, mere boys, are immediately snatched away (plate 21)[18] – both of these are motifs which directly recall

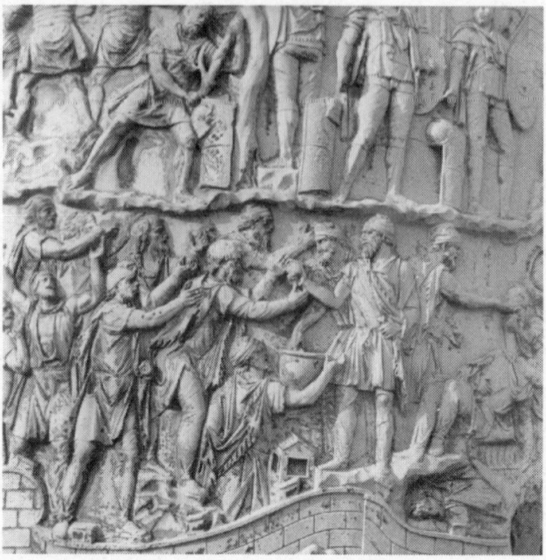

Plate 19

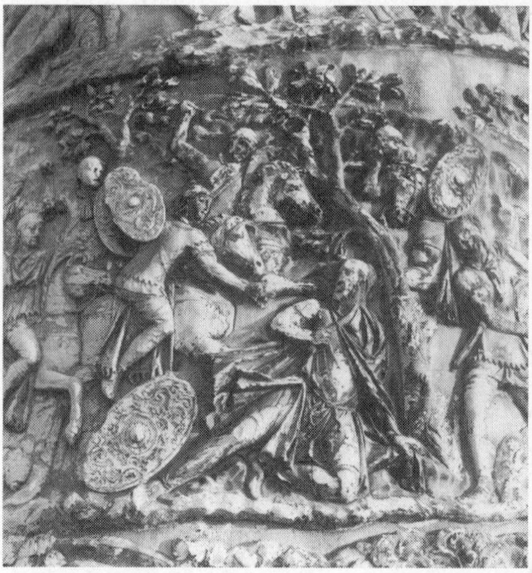

Plate 20

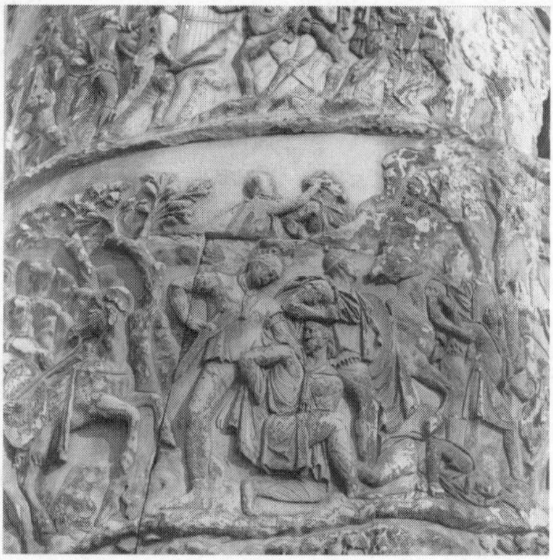

Plate 21

Plates 19–21: Trajan's Column, Rome

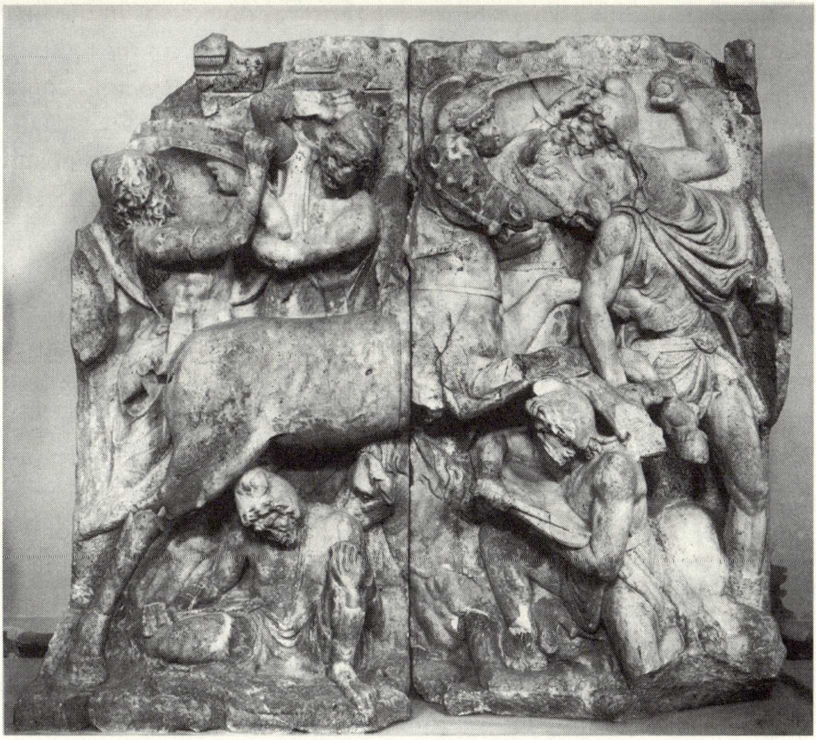

Plate 22: Scene from the Monument of Lucius Verus at Ephesos depicting the battle with the Parthians

the paintings in Pompey's triumphal procession with the death of Mithridates and his family.

Finally, there is the battle with the Parthians from the monument of Lucius Verus at Ephesos (after AD 169) (plate 22).[19] In the centre, the victorious Emperor in his chariot, quite unrealistically raised above the milling battlefield. Immediately in front of him, a soldier strikes down an Oriental, whose features are twisted and drawn backwards with pain; while in the hollow space beneath the horses, a whole still life of death unfolds: a collapsing man pulls a spear from a wound in his stomach, another plunges a sword into his chest, between them, the bulky form of a fallen horse. It is yet another glimpse of the fate of the individual, phrased in a language of forms that is Hellenistic in its origins.

The goal of this style of representation was obviously, in the first place, to enhance the glory of the victor by the pathos of the fighting and the suffering of the defeated. Secondly, the strain of victory could be brought out, at its most powerful, through the dynamic formal language of Hellenistic art. A fundamental Hellenistic experience, from the time of Alexander the Great onwards, had been that great undertakings, especially wars and conquests, go together with the greatest toils.[20] The physical and mental vigour developed in Hellenistic art sets before our eyes time and time again, and particularly in the battle-scenes, the triumph over toil (*ponos*). This ideological aspect also encouraged the adoption of such artistic forms in Rome: for here there was already a valid model in the concept of *labor*, which might find expression in similar form.[21] Even though, in Hellenistic and more especially in Roman Imperial times, rulers and commanders were progressively exempted from the tumult and toils of battle, the task of the army was nevertheless still strongly characterised by this concept.

Besides the congested battles between masses, Roman art also continued the portrayal, in a spacious ambience, of complicated military episodes such as the besieging of towns. This type of representation, evidently taken over from the Hellenistic tradition, was also given a specifically Roman function through its use in Republican political paintings.[22] It is attested in the written sources by the account of the topography (*situs*) and assaults (*oppugnationes*) in the picture of the capture of Carthage, which L. Hostilius Mancinus displayed and expounded during his bid for the consulship in 146 BC.[23] An echo of this mode of representation is preserved in a Pompeian wall-painting, in which the area of the town's amphitheatre is depicted, with a notorious riot between the inhabitants of Pompeii and of Nocera in AD 59 taking place there.[24] Above all, as is well known, the fighting scenes on the columns of Trajan and Marcus Aurelius, as well as on the Arch of Septimius Severus in Rome (AD 195–203), stand in this tradition.

This way of representation is even more clearly differentiated from Classical forms by the inclusion of the human figure in the ambience. But it too had the power, by depicting the setting of actions, to achieve something of central importance for the Roman mind: to show off the geographical conditions and levels of civilisation in which, and against which, the Roman army had asserted itself. Not least, therefore, this too was a depiction of *labor*.[25]

When applied to Roman state monuments, it is true, these Hellenistic traditions are placed in surroundings with a strong aura of quite different, Classical models. But this situation finds its parallel in Roman literature, on both a theoretical and a practical level. Lucian, in his treatise of the writing of history which closely follows the ideas of the Caesarean period, in general clearly represents the classicising position of Atticism; yet for the description of land- and sea-battles he admits embellishment of a more strongly poetic kind, which of course is not meant to break up his generally moderate style.[26] Historiographical practice proceeds similarly: Sallust, while preserving a severely Classical style, seized on the descriptive methods of Hellenistic historiography when it came to portraying a panic in Rome or a battlefield strewn with corpses.[27] Caesar, against the background of his sober commentary-style, chose forms of dramatic, eye-witness narrative for certain subjects and certain desired effects.[28] Livy, despite his generally classicising style, ventured on the possibilities of strongly persuasive effects for describing battles, sieges and plagues;[29] the same is true, to an even greater degree, of Tacitus.[30] As in the visual arts, heterogeneous models were initially chosen from the point of view of the subject-matter, and then integrated into as unified a style as possible.

NOTES

1. Zinserling (1959–60); Hölscher (1978), esp. 344ff.
2. See recently (and convincingly) Meyer (1983) 116ff.
3. Diod. Sic. 31.18.2.
4. Polyb. 6.15.8; Zinserling (1959–60) 414.
5. Compare Burck (1964) 197ff., who includes Hellenistic examples.
6. On what follows, see Hölscher (1980b), esp. 353ff.
7. App., *Mith.* 117; Zinserling (1959–60) 411f., no. 17.
8. Night-battles in Duris: Diod. Sic. 20.29; 20.65ff. Clash of arms and silence, for example in Sisenna (so roughly contemporary with Pompey's pictures): Peter (1914) Frr. 25, 26, 64. Compare already Diod. Sic. 20.7.4. Note also the frequent occurrence of war-trumpets in Hellenistic and Roman battle-scenes: Andreae (1956) 65ff.
9. See n. 7.

10. App., *B.Civ.* 2.101; Zinserling (1959–60) 412f., no. 18. Similarly spectacular will have been the portrayal of Cleopatra's end at Octavian's triumph after Actium: Dio Cass. 51.21.8. Zinserling (1959–60) 413, no. 20.
11. Scott Ryberg (1955), esp.144ff.; Helbig[4] II, no. 1670 (E. Simon); Hölscher (1985b), esp. 88f.; La Rocca (1985) 94f.
12. Palestrina relief: Kraus (1967), pl. 181b. Mantua frieze, chapter 3, n.12.
13. Kähler (1968).
14. Furtwängler (1900), pl. 60.
15. Pallottino (1938); Salis (1947) 100; Leander Touati (1987).
16. The figure made a special impression on Bianchi Bandinelli (1950), pls. 115, 213.
17. Lehmann-Hartleben (1926), pl. 57, cxx–cxxii. The column shows many such scenes, which repay closer study: here only a few examples will be picked out. Corresponding portrayals, but in a more piercing tone, can be found on the Marcus Column. Compare too, for example, Livy 28.22.
18. Lehmann-Hartleben (1926) pls. 67f., cxlv–cxlvi.
19. Vermeule (1968) 106; Eichler (1971) 109f.; Oberleitner *et al.* (1978) 82, no. 66.
20. Kleiner (1950–1), esp. 219ff.; Hölscher (1973) 174, 185, 222. For its development in Hellenistic times, see Hesberg (1987), esp. 119ff.
21. Compare Lau (1975) 26ff. for its relationship with *ponos*.
22. Above, p. 38, with literature in nn. 1ff.
23. Plin., *HN* 35.23; Zinserling (1959–60) 409f., no. 13.
24. Kähler (1958–60) pl. 148 upper, 233ff.
25. Lau (1975) 87ff.
26. Lucian, *Hist.Conscr.* 45. On this, see Avenarius (1956) 130ff.; Flach (1973) 35f. Compare too Homeyer (1965) 45ff.
27. Sall., *Cat.* 31.1–3; 61. On this, see Flach (1973) 37ff. Compare Gärtner (1986).
28. Mutschler (1975), esp. 52ff.
29. Burck (1964) 176ff., esp. 195ff.; Introduction, xxiiiff. Flach (1973) 41ff.
30. Flach (1973) 44ff. It is significant that Tac., *Ann.* 4.32, specifically cites military events as subjects for gripping historical narrative. For an example, the account of the fall and suicide of Otho: *Hist.* 2.46–9.

CHAPTER 6

State ceremonial: the tradition of Classical dignity

But even though Hellenistic forms of representation retained their validity in Rome as well, they were confined to certain subjects: overall, the tradition of the fifth and fourth centuries retained the upper hand. Much the same is true of historiography. Already Polybios, in a well-known rejoinder, had expressed opposition to the 'tragicising' movement in historical narrative,[1] though he was admittedly unable to prevent it from enjoying a continuation in Rome, with Coelius Antipater, Sisenna and others.[2] But by the mid-first century at the latest, Roman politicians had generated a fundamental resistance to these emotional types of literature and art. The motive behind this is clear from Cicero's critique of the emotional, so-called 'Asianic' movement in rhetoric, which would doubtless apply to 'tragic' historiography as well: it is that this style is incompatible with the *gravitas* and *auctoritas* of a Roman office-holder.[3] A rhetorical style is at the same time a political style; words are a reflection of the soul. We see in the political choice of Classicism an expression of the Roman order of state.

But the recourse to Classical Greek models was equally strongly dictated by subject-matter. Cicero's plea for the solemnity of the Classical Attic style of oratory is directed at the special case of Roman official dignity. In the field of statecraft Polykleitos, the great exponent of rational, Classical design, became exemplary in a special way with the first, programmatic ruler portrait of the Principate: that is, for the principal Augustan portrait-type created *ca.* 31 BC (plate 23), whose ageless features with plain surfaces, sharp edges and a balanced composition of crescent-shaped curls echo Polykleitos' Doryphoros (*ca.* 440 BC) (plate 24).[4] A striking illustration of how far the leaning towards Polykleitan models could go in the Augustan period is given by the

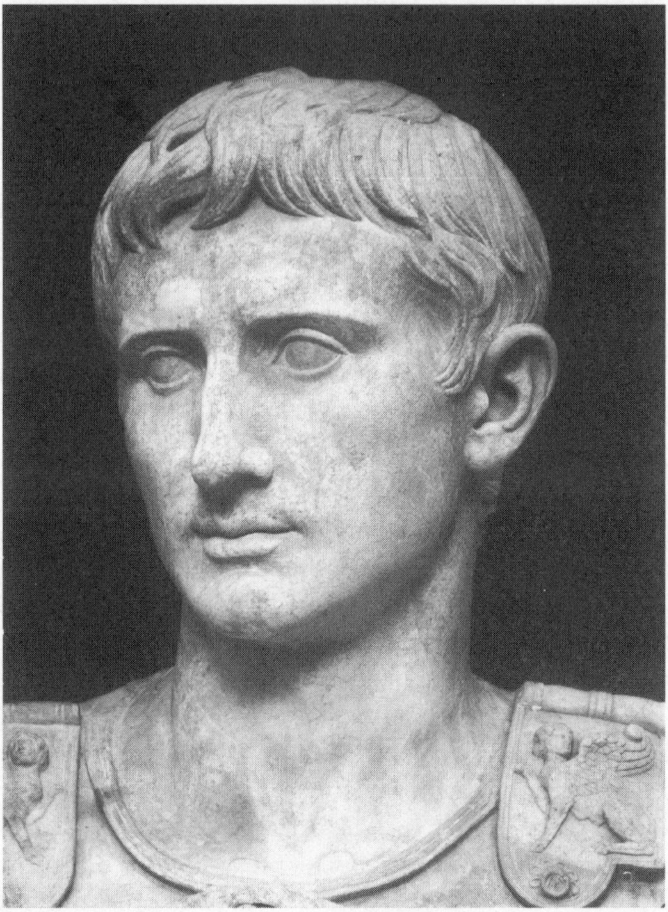

Plate 23: Head of statue of Augustus from Prima Porta, 19 BC

private portrait of a boy, in Bochum (last quarter first century BC) (plate 25).[5] If Quintilian saw the characteristics of *gravitas* and *sanctitas* in the Doryphoros,[6] these remained subject-specific qualities which, in the Roman context, applied especially to the ruler and the state as objects of reverence. How consciously thematic was this use of the model in question is shown by the portrait of Agrippa (*ca.* 30–20 BC) (plate 26), which had at the same time to express the dynamic of the military commander, and which therefore carried on the Hellenistic tradition.[7]

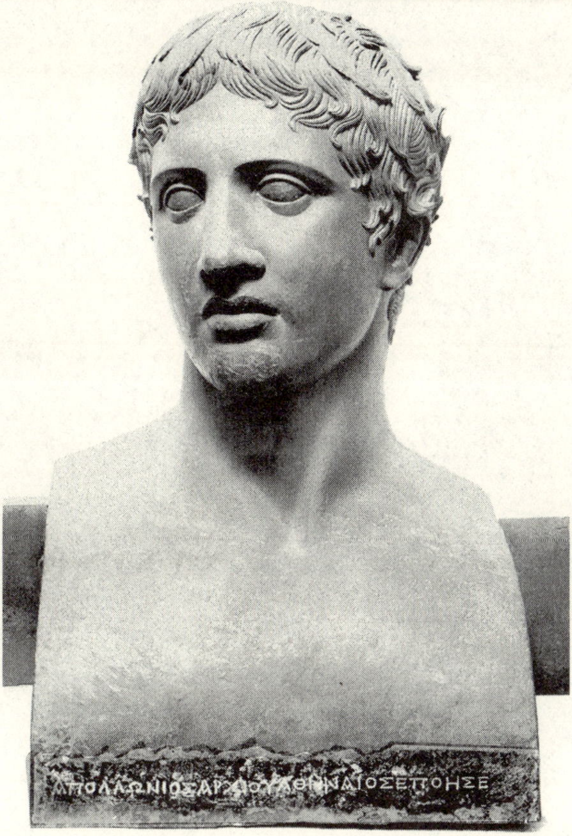

Plate 24: Herm-copy of the Doryphoros by Polykleitos

Much the same is true of the great processional frieze on the enclosing wall of the Ara Pacis (13–9 BC), which represents the solemn foundation ceremony with the Emperor, high office bearers and the Imperial family.[8] One might certainly question whether the arrangement of the procession, which runs round the building in two columns facing the entrance, is to be understood as a direct reference back to the Parthenon frieze (447–432 BC); for the Parthenon is not unique in this respect[9] and the designers of the Ara Pacis may also have been simply following a continuous tradition. On the other hand, the formal resemblances to the Parthenon frieze and other Classical reliefs

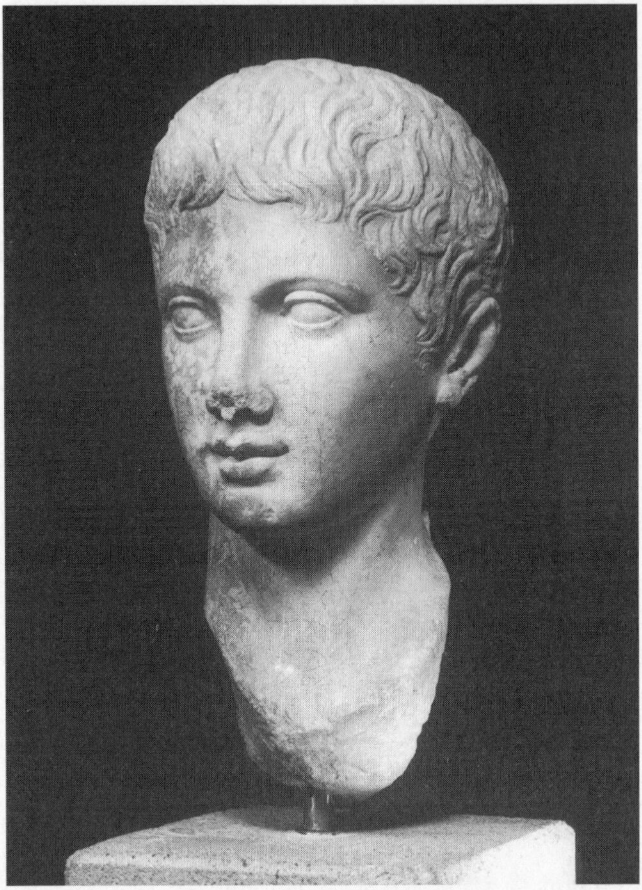

Plate 25: Head of boy, last quarter first century BC

are obvious. The composition of the figures on the Ara Pacis is exceptionally close to the Classical frieze: in the planar arrangement of the figures which, in the rear plane of the relief, are in part so shallow that they seem to merge into the background; and in the breaking up of the procession by figures facing backwards, joining in conversation with their neighbours (plates 27; 28).[10] Single figures of the Ara Pacis also follow Classical types very closely; for men in togas, especially, the relaxed ceremonial bearing of the figures on the Parthenon frieze and similar reliefs presented itself as a good model, especially as the

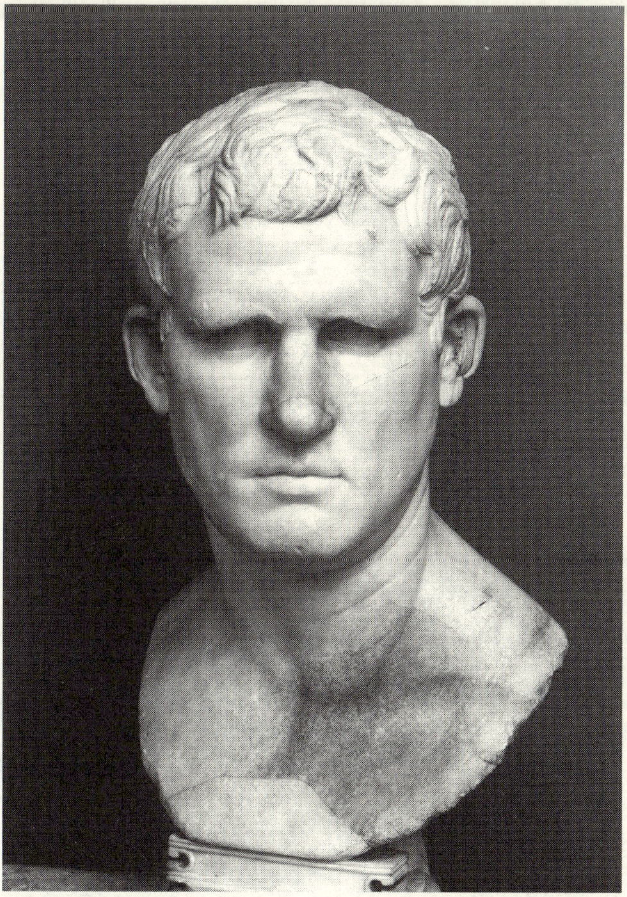

Plate 26: Head of Agrippa, *ca.* 30–20 BC

costume required only slight alterations in comparison with the Greek *himation*, or outer garment (plates 29; 30).[11] With this, too, were often associated specific details in the arrangement of the drapery: on the *togati* (those dressed in togas), there appear fold-lines, bulges and build-ups of material, which resemble Classical reliefs surprisingly closely (plates 31 and 29; 30).[12]

All these features appear on the Ara Pacis not in pure Classical form, but interspersed with later elements;[13] yet the fundamental – and also intentional – relationship with the Greek High Classical style cannot

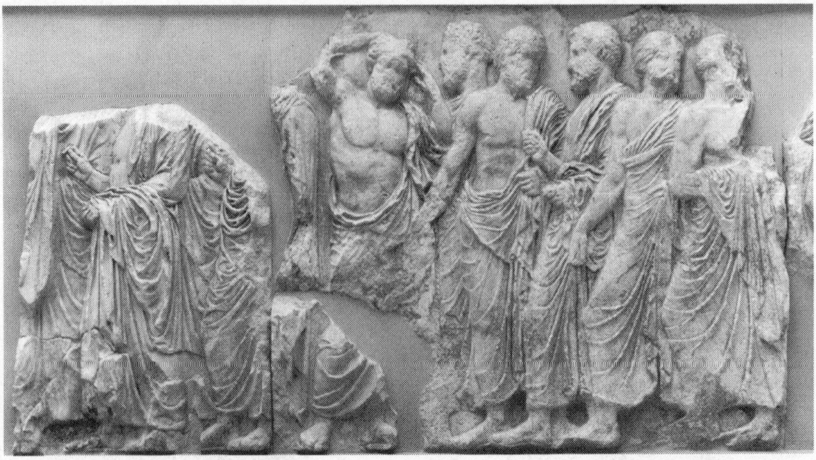

Plate 27: Parthenon frieze, detail

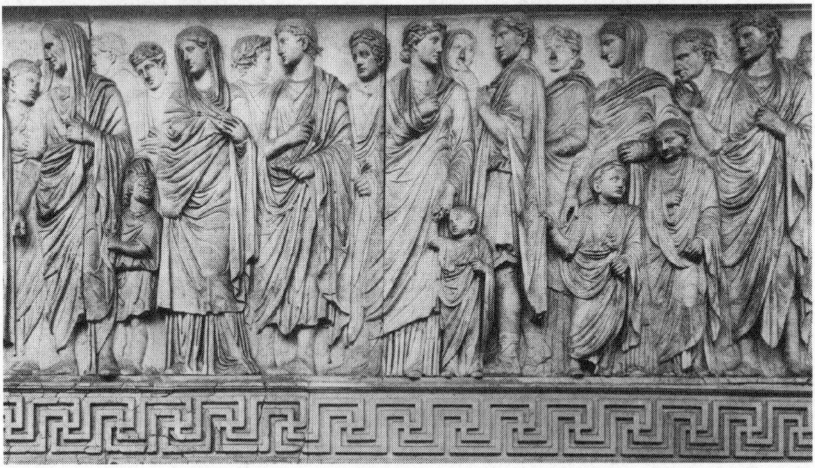

Plate 28: Ara Pacis, South frieze, detail

be doubted. Its language of forms is adopted here for the development of a new style of representation, in which the chief figures of the state might be shown in appropriate dignity at a solemn ceremony. In Roman eyes, the style of Pheidias embodied such concepts as *maiestas*, *pondus* and *auctoritas*; these qualities stand close beside the *gravitas* and *sanctitas* of Polykleitos. Together they fulfil Cicero's demand for *dignitas*.

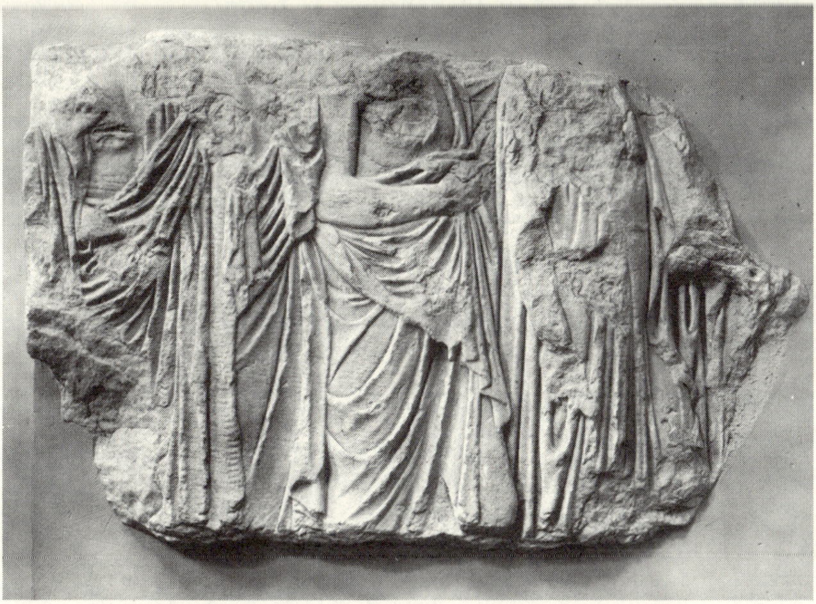

Plate 29: Parthenon frieze, detail

In this, as is well known, we may discern a prominent attitude of Augustus, which strongly shaped both his real-life manner and his political style.[14] By his Classicism he openly distinguished himself from Antony, whom he accused of 'Asianic' tendencies in his style of oratory, designed to elicit more amazement than insight:[15] a confrontation, therefore, between intellect and emotion. He sought to restore the *dignitas* of the priesthoods and the Senate and, in the same spirit, took care that in the hub of public life, the Forum, only the toga should be worn.[16] In his own person, he displayed an ideal of calm serenity and cheerfulness, and his style of speech appears to have been correspondingly elegant and temperate.[17]

But just as this was very much Augustus' overall personal style, so it was equally clearly concentrated on certain areas: on the Senate, the most prominent priesthoods and, above all, on his own person. This is confirmed by his literary taste: he liked to listen to the whole possible range of talent and its decidedly heterogeneous products; but where he himself was the subject, he appreciated only writing that was

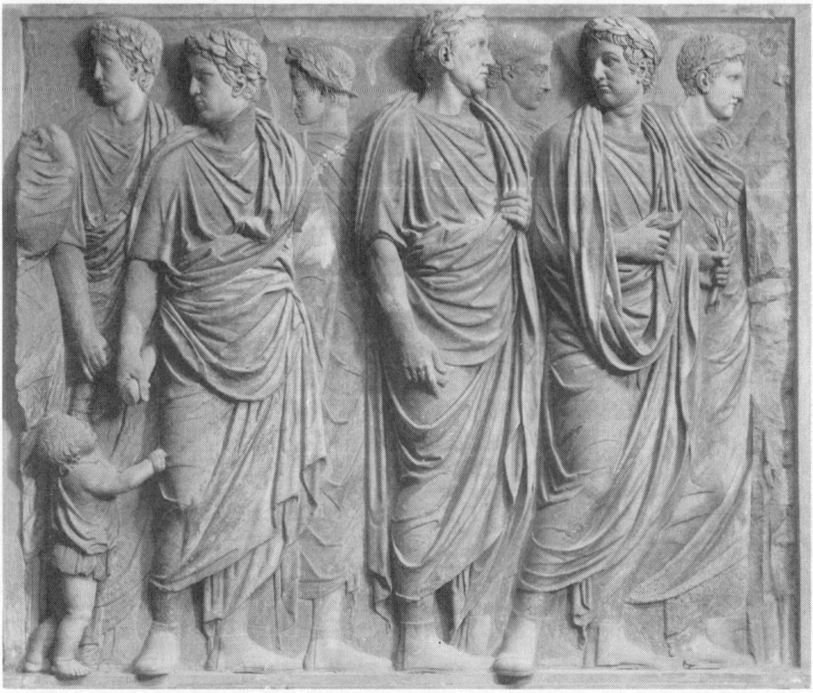

Plate 30: Ara Pacis, North frieze, detail

serious and at the same time distinguished[18] – and so comparable to the great frieze of the Ara Pacis.

The Classical Greek style was, however, put to use with changes of meaning: for the depiction of *dignitas* and *auctoritas*, that is for ideas that belonged firmly to the core of the Roman system of values. Hence the concept of Classicism applies only on a limited scale here: art is not displaying a general, historicising backwards turn towards Classical Athens; it is rather expressing the new situation of Rome and the Empire, alive to the present and looking to the future. Only in this light does the further tradition of this style of representation become intelligible.

The subject of a solemn state ceremony was, it seems, so persuasively embodied by the form of composition used in the great frieze of the Ara Pacis that, despite changes in the actual events portrayed, it

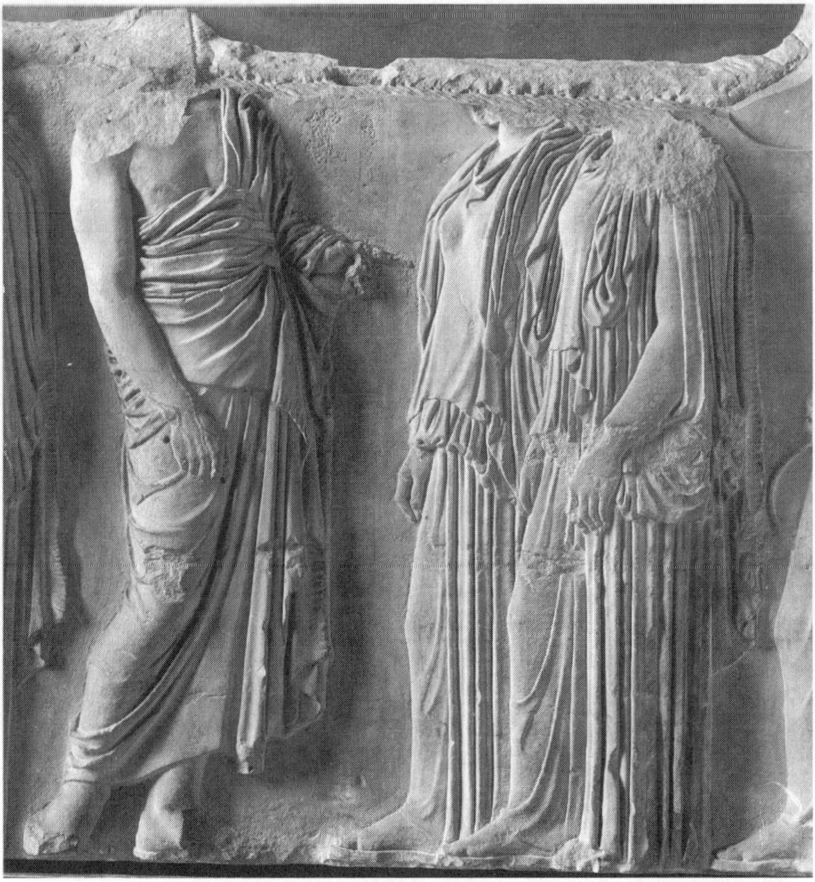

Plate 31: Parthenon frieze, detail

retained its fundamental validity for centuries: the great relief scenes of the so-called Ara Pietatis (AD 41–54), of the Arch of Titus (after AD 81), of the Arch of Trajan at Beneventum (AD 109–14) and of the triumphal arch of Marcus Aurelius (after AD 176) form an unbroken chain from the Ara Pacis.[19] It is all the more revealing, therefore, that this tradition underwent very substantial modifications through the changes in marble-working techniques and concepts of relief-sculpture – that is, through the developments in temporal style.[20] As a result, the appearance of these representations moved further and further away from the forms of Classical Greek relief. On the Arch of Beneventum, the figures stand in the round, against a neutral background, as if on a stage; they appear to be crowded together and ranged in depth; deep grooves make the figures and drapery rich in contrasts, thereby securing their effect; none of this can any longer call up associations with the Parthenon frieze. Clearly the style of representation of the *dignitas* of state ceremony, having originally come into being with the help of Greek Classicism, soon developed a far-reaching independence: direct references back to Classical Greek forms were no longer required; the tradition had acquired enough weight, independently of its origins, to communicate the desired message, regardless of all temporal changes, in its own right.

NOTES

1. Polyb. 2.56.
2. Peter (1914) 158ff., 276ff. Flach (1973) 26ff.
3. Cic., *Brut.* 95, 327. Compare Dion. Hal., *Orat.vett.* 3.1: Atticising rhetoric would meet the requirements and the *arete* of the men of power and influence (the *dunasteuontes*). 'Asianic' rhetoric, by contrast, lacks *gravitas* and is unsuited to the good statesman: Cic., *Brut.* 95.325–37. Dion. Hal., *Orat.vett.* 1.4. On this, see Gelzer in *Classicisme*, 16f., 21ff. For the transference of these categories from rhetoric to historiography, compare Dion. Hal., *Comp.* 4.30, who counts Duris (and admittedly Polybios too) as part of the emotional tendency. Compare Gelzer in *Classicisme*, 29. Additionally, Dion. Hal., *Ant.Rom.* 1.1.3: Gelzer in *Classicisme*, 22.
4. For its interpretation, see above all Zanker (1973) 44ff.
5. Imdahl and Kunisch (1979) 36ff.
6. Quint., *Inst.* 5.12.20. Zanker (1973).
7. Johansen (1971) 17–48.
8. For the stylistic analysis which follows, see especially Borbein (1975), esp. 252ff. Compare also Kleiner (1978).
9. The Parthenon frieze as model: Borbein (1975) 252ff. A later example is the grave-monument of Metrodoros of Chios in Berlin: Studniczka (1888), esp. 199ff., pl. 3. Conze and Puchstein (1891) 288ff., no. 766 A.
10. Borbein (1975), 254f. Above, p. 15.
11. Compare Moretti (1948) 13, fig. 2 with Brommer (1977) pls. 58, 64; also Diepolder (1931) pl. 14. Also Simon (1967) pls. 16–19 with Brommer (1977) pls. 150f., 156, 168, 171.

12. Compare Simon (1967) pls. 16 lower, 17, 19 upper with Brommer (1977) pls. 150, 166, 183, 186. Also Borbein (1975) 254.
13. See below, pp. 77ff.
14. Zanker (1983) 27ff.
15. Suet., *Aug*. 86.
16. Suet., *Aug*. 31, 35, 40.
17. Suet., *Aug*. 79, 86.
18. Suet., *Aug*. 89.
19. Hamberg (1945) 46ff., esp. 99ff. 'Ara Pietatis': Torelli (1982) figs. III 20ff. Arch of Titus: Pfanner (1983) pls. 45, 54. Arch of Trajan at Beneventum: Hassel (1966). Arch of Marcus Aurelius: Scott Ryberg (1967).
20. For what follows, see similarly Borbein (1975) 259f.

CHAPTER 7

The semantic system: the elements and their use

The phenomena we have studied are part of a system. Each of the two iconographic themes, the solemn state ceremony and the battle, shows clearly that specific types of representation, from different epochs of Greek art, were chosen for specific subjects. The underlying assumption is obviously that, in each successive period, convincing possibilities of representation had been found for each particular subject. This range of representation certainly allowed the relevant historical events, with their specific features, to be differentiated and made recognisable; yet each of the two traditions of the congested battlefield and the prestigious ceremony coheres so closely that, in a wider sense, we can speak of patterns of scenic representation. These formal patterns, at the same time, also gave expression to a certain imagined conception of the events represented: state ceremonies were shown as being conducted with religious or official dignity, battles portrayed in terms of pathos, emotion and straining effort. The choice of the form was thus based on the content.

That this is a fundamental principle of Roman art could be demonstrated only by detailed examination of individual groups of subjects. A few readily available examples of idealising figures can at least indicate that some kind of system is present.

The Augustan altar in Arezzo (first quarter first century AD) shows, on its frontal face, the She-Wolf, the Twins and the Shepherds in a landscape setting of Hellenistic origin; on the side-faces, by contrast, there are two 'neo-Attic' victory figures, one archaising, the other in the tradition of the 'Rich Style' (plates 3, 32, 33).[1] In such a context, both figures demonstrate the fact that the 'neo-Attic' style is neither a constitutive style of specific workshops nor a reflection of the general

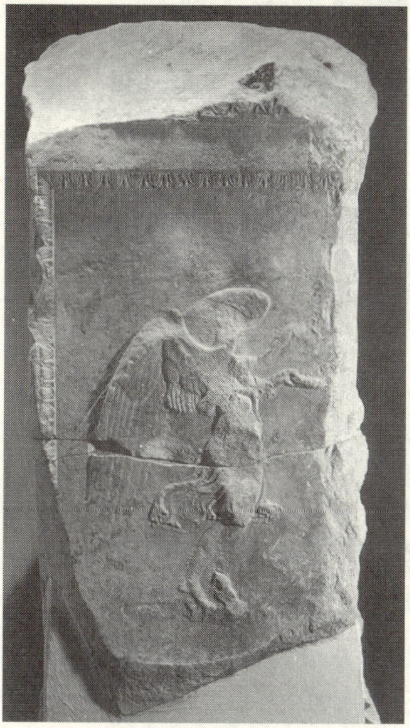

Plate 32

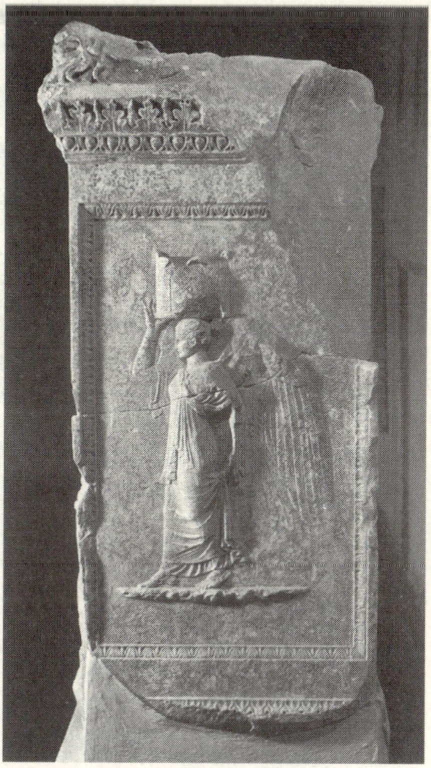

Plate 33

Plates 32–33: Side-faces of altar depicting Victories, Augustan period

taste of specific clients, but that it primarily represents a specific form for specific functions – in this case, specific subjects – alongside other forms which could serve other functions. Just as Hellenistic landscape was appropriate for the primitive idyll, so the 'neo-Attic' style, with its vignette-like isolation of figures, served for abstract personifications, and its capricious elegance for their girlish quality.[2]

FIGURES IN THE ROUND

With sculpture in the round, the borrowing of forms from Polykleitos and the circle of Lysippos is instructive. Polykleitos' works, it

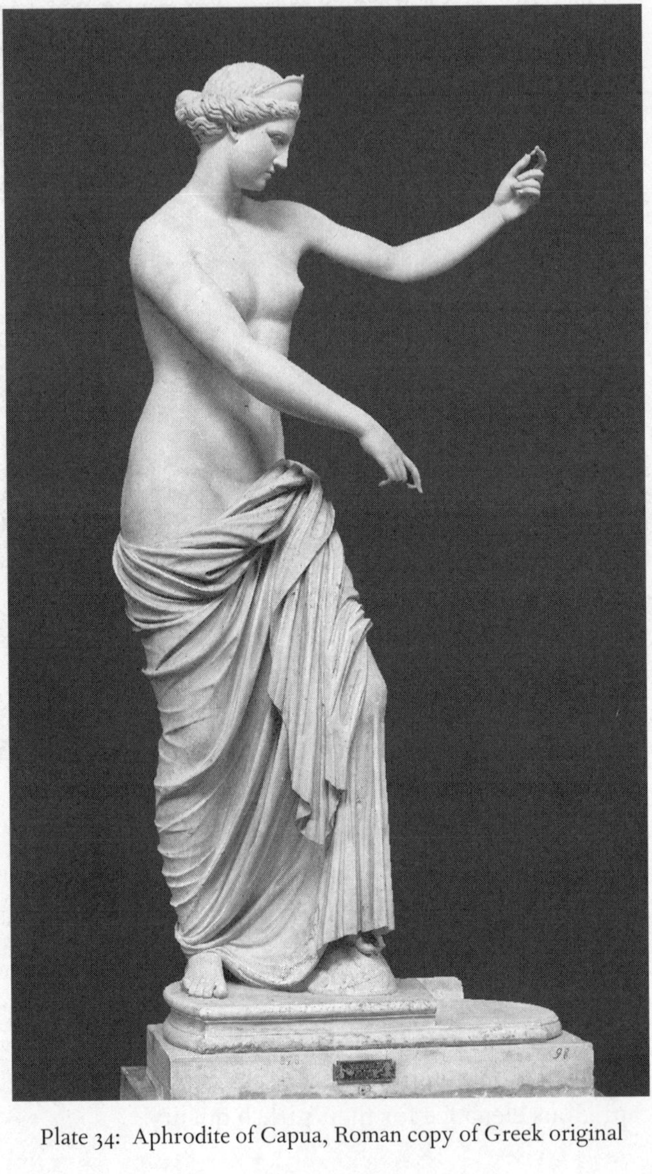

Plate 34: Aphrodite of Capua, Roman copy of Greek original

seems, served especially for those figures from the world of mythology and the gods who had a physique of idealised beauty as one of their characteristics. In accordance with this, Quintilian praises Polykleitos because he lent the human form 'a beauty that transcended reality' (*decor supra verum*).[3] The Perseus in Copenhagen (*ca.* AD 130–50), based on Polykleitos' 'Doryphoros', is a good example.[4] The Lysippan head-type of the Ares Ludovisi (*ca.* 330–300 BC), on the other hand, was later employed above all for figures of Hermes.[5] Evidently the agility of this god, in his athletic aspects, was better reflected in the language of Lysippos and Praxiteles: Quintilian says of them, in confirmation, 'that they had most satisfactorily come close to reality' (*ad veritatem accessisse optime*).[6] A more precise investigation of these questions would have to range far and wide. Here, three further examples may suffice for clarification.

Among Greek female figures, the Aphrodite of Capua type (plate 34) of the late fourth century BC had especially diverse influence: the goddess being portrayed looking at the reflection of her half-exposed body in the shield of Ares, and perhaps originally forming the cult-statue of the famous Temple of Aphrodite on Akrocorinth.[7] Here it is especially clear that the basis for the reception was iconographic and subject-related, in particular because of the placing of the arms wide apart.

Adaptations can be found from the mid-second century BC onwards. In the Venus de Milo (*ca.* 150 BC), the model is reworked to fit a new type of action, which can no longer be reconstructed;[8] the decisive factor, however, was doubtless the lost attribute, which fitted the pose of the arms.

With the transformation into the goddess of Victory, shown recording on a shield the fame of a victor, the subject-based motivation is unequivocal. The inscribing Nike is already a motif in the fourth century BC;[9] likewise, it was a practice going back to Classical times to use the surface of a shield for a representative victory inscription.[10] The fusion of both motifs, in the form of a goddess of Victory writing on a shield, is found on gems and on glass-paste, in various forms from, at the latest, the second century BC onwards: sitting, standing, or with a foot propped up.[11] For artists who knew how to handle older

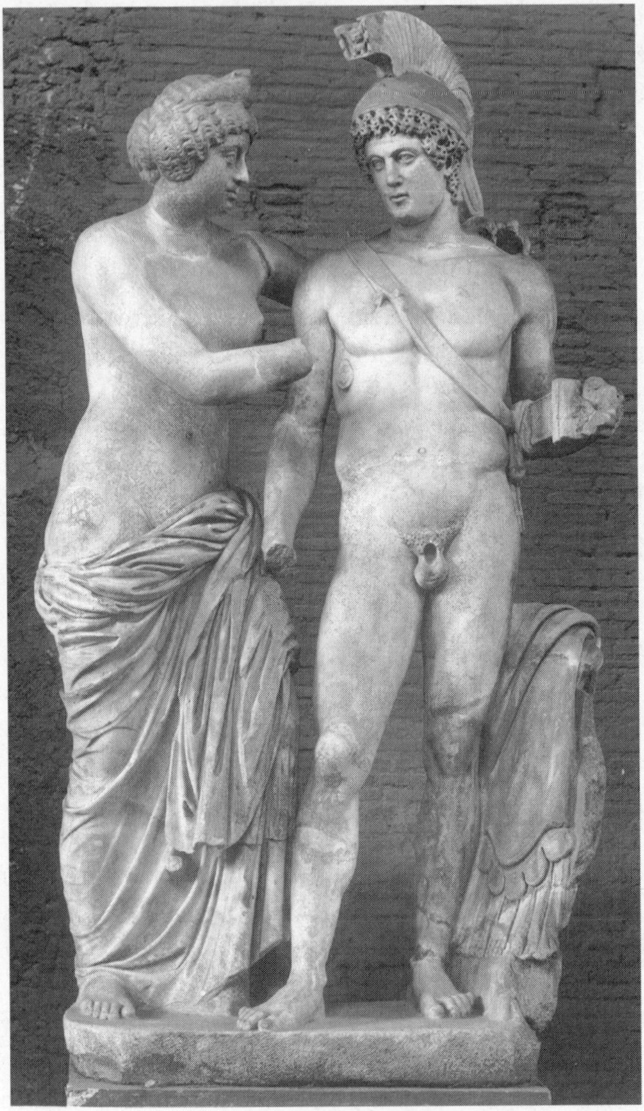

Plate 35: Portrait Group as Venus and Mars, Antonine period

figural subjects, the use of the Capua type for this subject immediately suggested itself. A gem which is certainly of Republican date and may belong to around 100 BC,[12] and which doubtless derives from some larger-scale representation, is testimony to this: the transformation of the Capua type into a goddess of Victory thus must have been carried out in the period of the Venus de Milo. The sketchy reproduction on the gem does not allow us to detect whether the body and drapery of the model were faithfully reproduced or more freely adapted there; but in any case we can recognise in this work a very experienced eye for the possibilities of reusing a Classical statue-type for a new subject.

By early Imperial times at the latest the type, in its goddess of Victory version, acquired a new topicality, with the now more exact borrowing of the body and drapery of the original. A famous example is the bronze statue from Brescia (*ca.* AD 50),[13] which originally had no wings but was nevertheless writing on a shield, and was thus a combination of Venus and Victoria together; later follow the relief figures, unambiguously characterised as Victories, on the Columns of Trajan and Marcus Aurelius. Caesar, already, had honoured his divine ancestress Venus as *Genetrix* and *Victrix* ('Mother' and 'Victorious') simultaneously, and identified her with the *Victoria Caesaris* ('Victory of Caesar'); for Augustus and his successors, Venus remained closely associated with the goddess of Victory. This association found a plausible iconographic formulation through the borrowing of an Aphrodite type to represent Victoria.

Yet other, equally content-derived, reasons were decisive in the reuse of the Capua type for representations of Mars and Venus. A series of examples are known from the Antonine period, where the group is used for portraits following the form of the two deities (plate 35). But probably the composition, also for Mars and Venus themselves, was a creation already of Augustan times.[14] For the War-God, the High Classical model of the Ares Borghese of Alkamenes (*ca.* 430 BC) was revived (plate 36).[15] The physical forms of this statue represented that divine weightiness and majesty, *pondus* and *auctoritas*, for which Quintilian praises this artist;[16] in his pose with lowered head, besides,

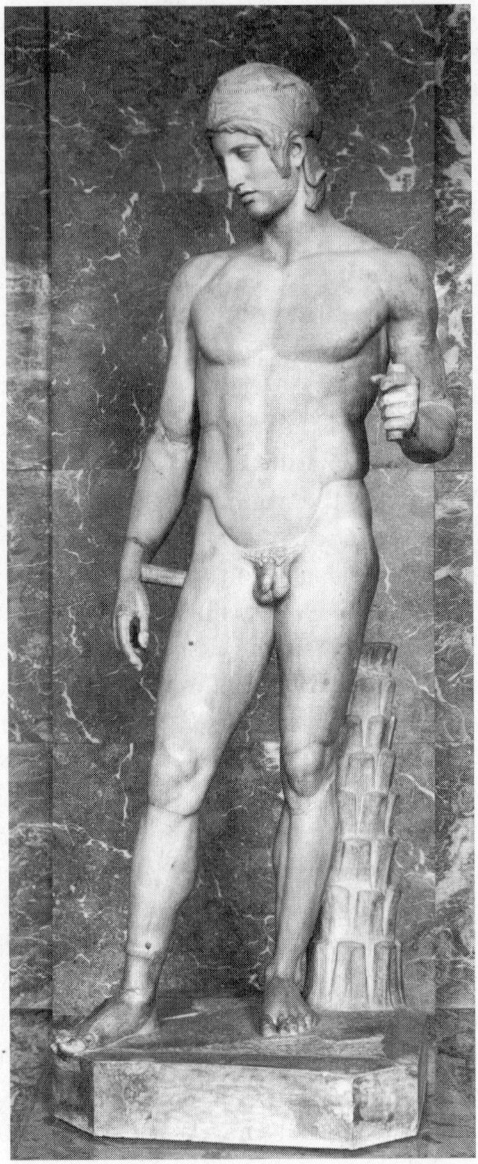

Plate 36: Ares Borghese, Roman copy of Greek original

the sentimental notion of his conquest by Venus could find expression. For the Love-Goddess, on the other hand, the Capua type at once suggested itself because of the position of its arms, which could easily be converted into an embrace. A further and perhaps even stronger reason was the baring of the body: as Mars' lover, Venus could at that period scarcely have been convincingly represented in any other way. Under this condition, models could only be found from the fourth century BC onwards, for only then did a taste for female nudity come to develop.[17] This choice of heterogeneous models for the new group arises plausibly from considerations of subject and motif. The success of the composition shows that a provenance from different epochs was not felt to be a disturbing discrepancy.

The range of borrowed Greek styles is extended by the copiously attested group of Bacchus with a Satyr from *ca.* AD 180–200 (plate 37).[18] For the god, one type, developed from the Late Classical figure of Apollo Lykeios (340–330 BC) (plate 38), was especially appropriate: the gesture of the arm resting on the head expressed the quiet calm amid wild surroundings, and at the same time the epiphanic exposure of the soft, sensual body, which are both characteristic of Bacchus. But if the setting of the Bacchic revel was to be included in the picture, then the usual choice was rather for a satyr of Hellenistic type; it was precisely this contrast with the ugliness of the half-animal youth with his crude, muscular body, restive pose and voyeuristic glance, that put the god into the limelight. Here again, the possibilities offered by the forms of two different periods were used for a contrast of subjects, in mutual relationship.

But this type alone could certainly not cover the whole range of the god's nature. Once the representation of the primitive aspect of his cult arose, the natural choice was for an archaising type. In this spirit, Late Archaic and Severe Style traits are combined in a figure in the Villa Albani (AD 140–60) (plate 39).[19] This makes clear that the different Greek styles were in no way mechanically tied to specific subjects, but that they were seen as being expressive of specific qualities. If a god had several aspects to his nature, as Bacchus did, then one could perfectly well use different patterns of representation too.

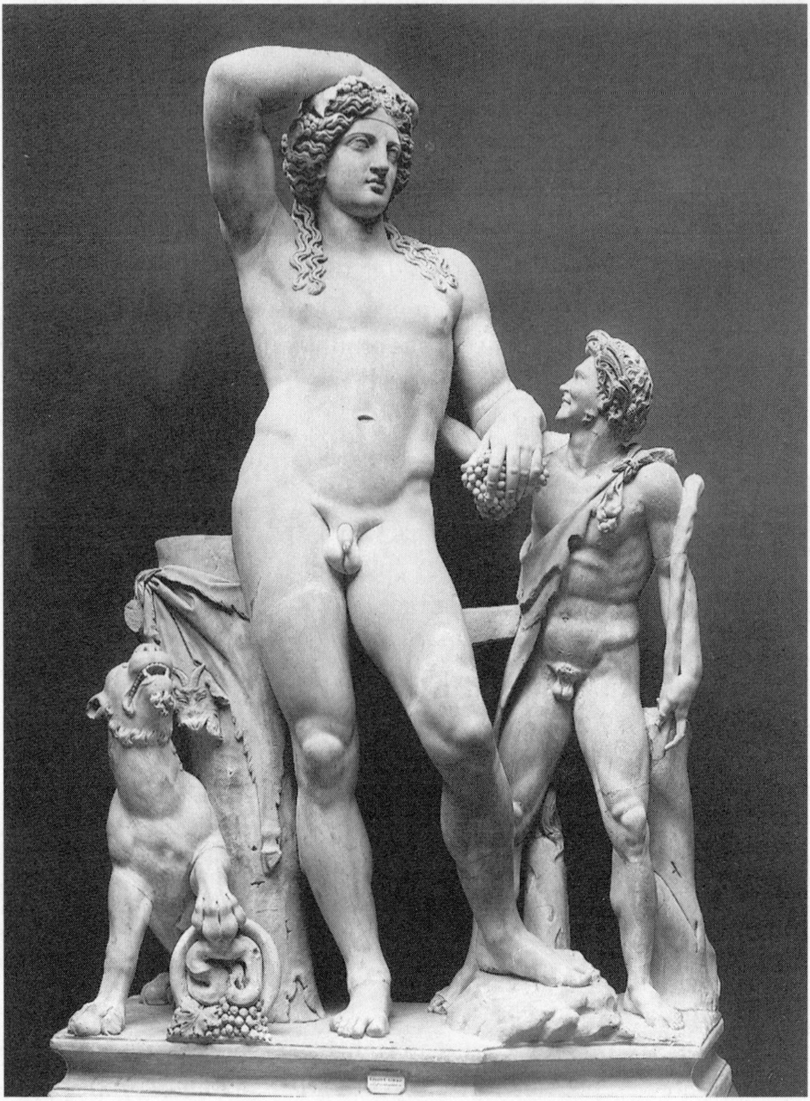

Plate 37: Group of Bacchus and Satyr, *ca.* AD 180–200

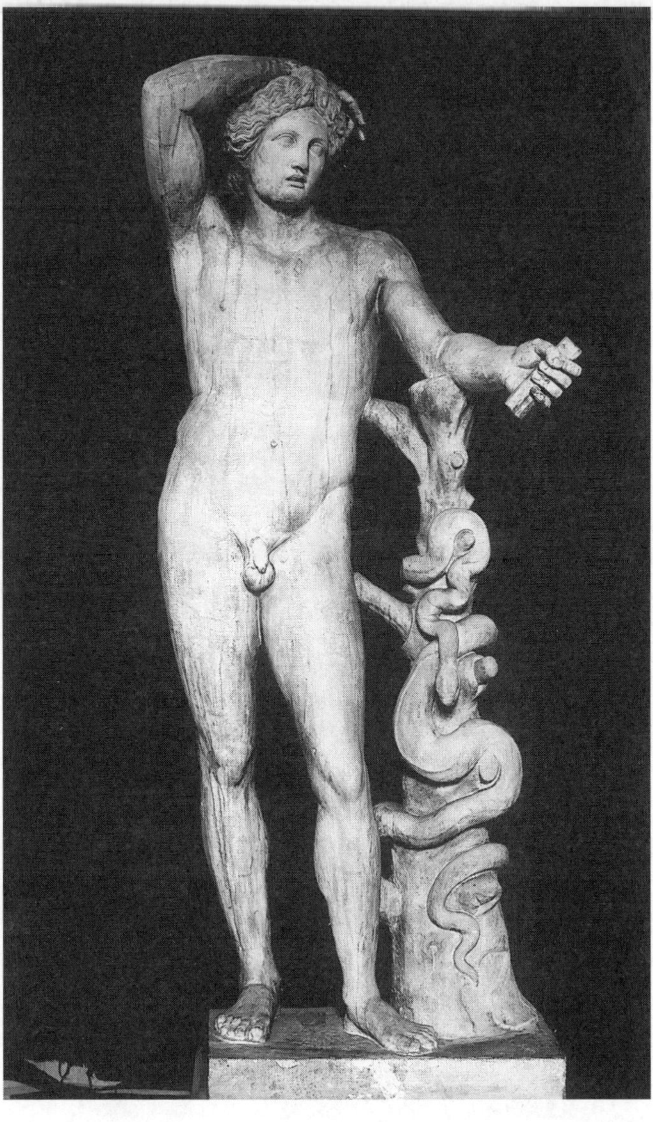

Plate 38: Apollo Lykeios, Roman copy of Greek original by Praxiteles

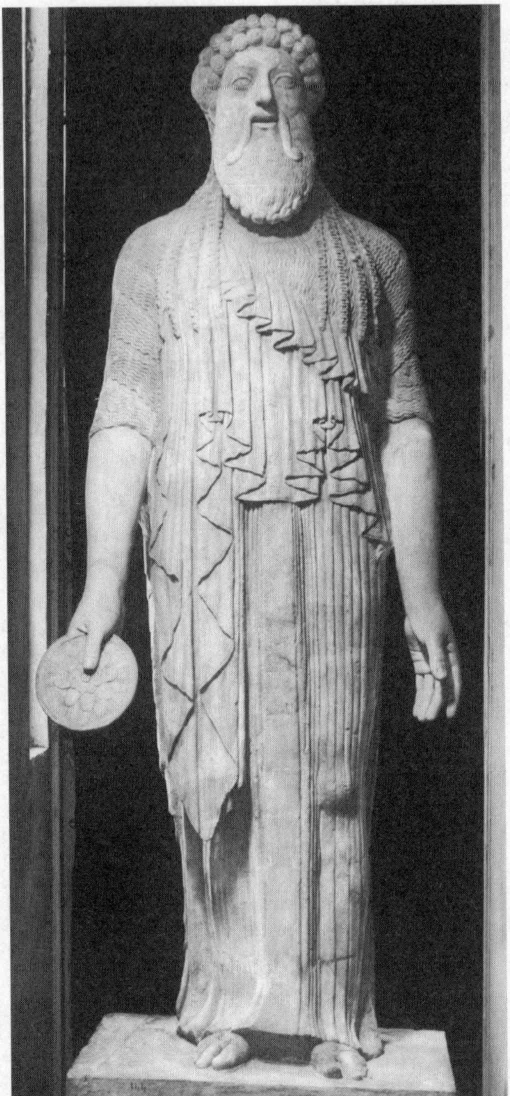

Plate 39: Statue of Bacchus in archaising style,
AD 140–60

This is very well brought out by the figures of Antinoös, which borrow and adapt older models for the body. The largest group dating back to AD 130–8 (plate 40) follows the type of the Tiber Apollo (*ca.* 450 BC) from the Severe Style,[20] which best catches the awkward charm of the age between ephebe and young man, usually linked with that incarnation of sensuous fullness which the Hadrianic age so cherished in figures of youths. It is telling that two of these figures are characterised as Bacchus, either by accessories on the supports or by attributes;[21] for the borrowing of the Tiber Apollo type, therefore, it was not its iconographic meaning that was decisive, but the idealised body-type in general terms. If Antinoös was to appear as an especially noble youth, on the other hand, then one might choose the Doryphoros of Polykleitos from the mid-fifth century, again remodelled with the ampler, tangible bodily ideal of this boy in mind, as on a statue in Naples (plate 41).[22] If, again, the emphasis were on the epiphanic radiance of the youth, and on his kinship with youthful deities like Apollo and Bacchus, then the Apollo Lykeios type of the later fourth century could be substituted, as in a statue from Lepcis Magna (plate 42).[23] And for portrayal as a dancing satyr, as in a figure in the Conservatori Palace (plate 43), the spiral dancer-figures of Hellenistic times supplied the model.[24] Thus the choice of types from different Greek stylistic phases allowed different aspects of the nature of the same figure to be stressed. But here again, it is the subject-matter which is decisive for the choice of model.

All in all, it is clear – to round the picture off – that for traditionally dignified figures of gods and heroes, the noble forms of High Classicism, even of the Late Archaic or Severe Style, were preferred; for soaring or dancing figures like Victories or maenads, the vibrant forms of the 'Rich Style' of the late fifth century; while, for epiphanic deities like Apollo, Bacchus or Venus, models of the fourth century were very often chosen; for agile athletes and the nimble Mercury, works in the Lysippan tradition; for satyrs or giants, Hellenistic ones. None of this, obviously, is without exceptions, nor a matter of binding rules; but as a tendency, it is none the less clear.

Two larger complexes of figural art should show the diversity and sophistication with which this visual language could be applied.

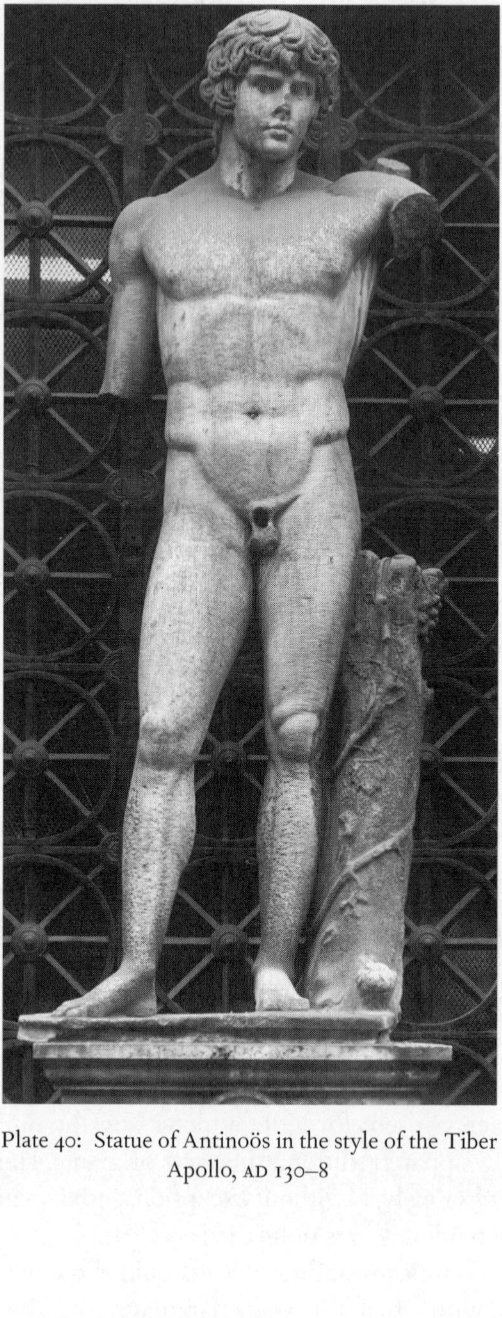

Plate 40: Statue of Antinoös in the style of the Tiber Apollo, AD 130–8

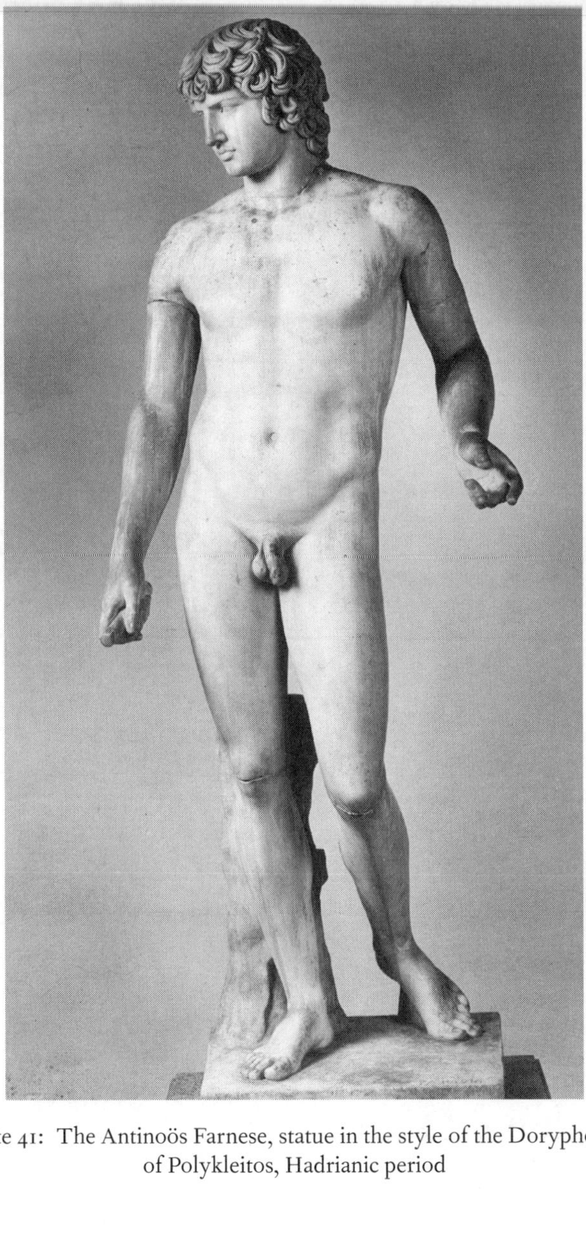

Plate 41: The Antinoös Farnese, statue in the style of the Doryphoros of Polykleitos, Hadrianic period

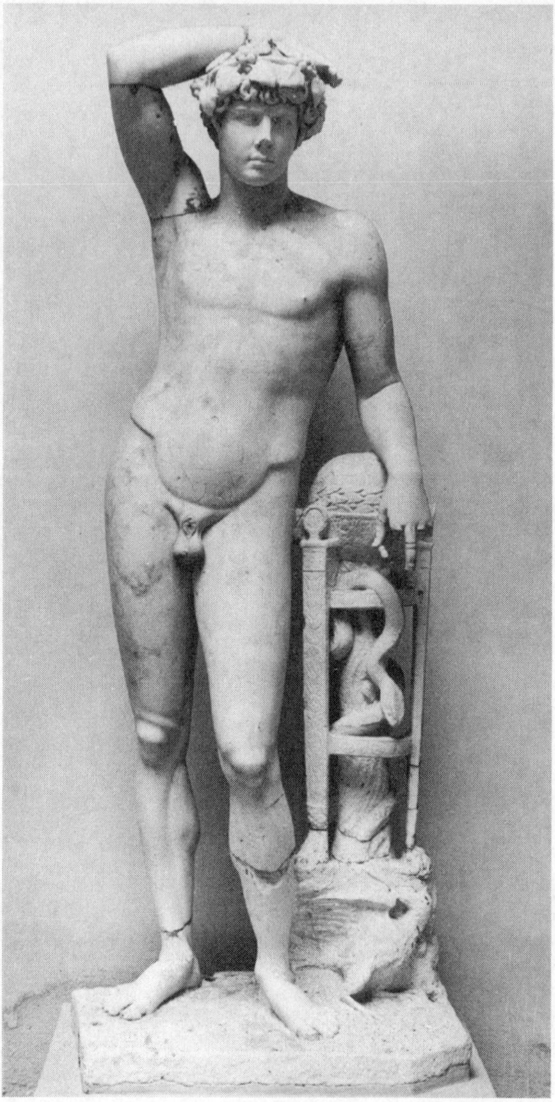

Plate 42: Statue of Antinoös in the style of the Apollo Lykeios, Hadrianic period

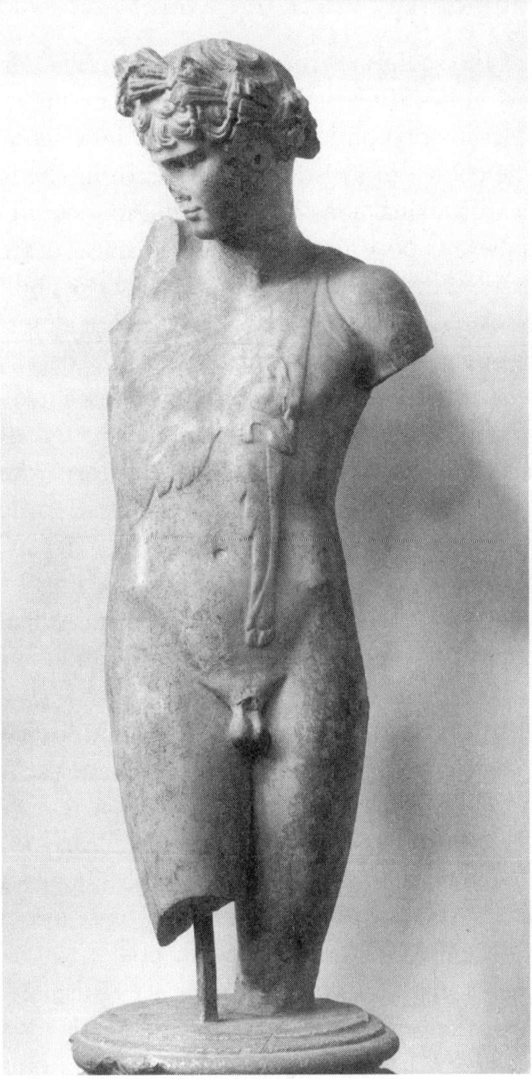

Plate 43: Statue of Antinoös portrayed as a dancing satyr, Hadrianic period

THE DÉCOR OF THE VILLA DEI PAPIRI (*CA.* 30 BC–AD 10)

The design of the sculptural furnishing of the Villa dei Papiri near Herculaneum follows a purely subject-based programme,[25] as an antithetic combination of political activity and intellectually pleasing seclusion. The choice of artistic models, accordingly, is geared not primarily towards formal considerations, but to those of content.

For the numerous portraits of Greek statesmen, orators, philosophers and poets, there was in any case neither possibility nor good reason for choosing according to stylistic taste. For almost all of them, there was but one portrait-type available. And the decisive thing was not the form, but the subject: the portrait must guarantee authenticity.

More informative are the idealised figures. The few divine statues show, by their Classical, at times even Archaic form, their authority as guiding figures for this view of life. In the large garden-peristyle, a bust of Athena forms the centrepiece of the extensive gallery of famous representatives of politics and intellectual life.[26] She could be no better represented than in the style of Classical Athens, acclaimed as the prototype of a revered and glorious association of the state and the intellect.

From the garden-peristyle, too, comes a head in Archaic-to-Severe Style which, from its juxtaposition with a poetess (or Muse?), probably represents Apollo.[27] The god was apparently to embody, through his Late Archaic forms, the ornate splendour of early Greek poetry; his devotee by contrast, with her Late Classical appearance, was to articulate the succession, from the viewpoint of a more personal and intimate understanding of what it is to be a poet.

The Athena Promachos which stood at the vanishing-point of the *tablinum* follows the forms of Late Archaic.[28] In this room, representatives of Greek *paideia* stood opposite exemplars of Roman *pietas* and *nobilitas*: on one side, Demosthenes and Epicurus as models of the art of political oratory and of personal philosophy, and with them two young men of Greek type; on the other, portraits of Romans, a *flamen* among them. The goddess who holds together these two worlds of national ideals is warlike, as are the Palladion in Athens and her counterpart in Rome. The antiquated forms recall the great epoch of the first heroic victories of the Greeks over the Persians, which were once again celebrated under Augustus as a model for political and cultural self-assertion.[29]

With them in the *tablinum* appear the two youths, embodiments of the ideal Greek conception of man in its two aspects: the short-haired athlete[30] and the beautiful, long-haired ephebe.[31] Both examples of Greek cultural education are portrayed in the style of that Classical epoch which was generally perceived as representing the summit of Greek culture. Yet at the same time the ideal of the 'perfect man' (*kalos kai agathos*) is so subtly differentiated that beauty and grace are characterised in post-Pheidian Attic form, athletic capacity in that of the school of Polykleitos.

There is a comparable juxtaposition, in a smaller side-room, of a bearded bust which probably represents Dionysos as the god of an ideal life of reverie, perhaps of mysticism,[32] and of Herakles as a model for the active life-style.[33] The god acquires a primeval dignity through the forms of early Classicism, the hero is a copy after Polykleitos, who gave form to the highest ideal of heroic *aretē*. A similar significance is also to be found in the well-known pair of busts of the Polykleitan Doryphoros and a corresponding female figure, which were exhibited in the peristyle, alongside portraits of Greeks that are difficult to interpret.[34] Probably Achilles and Penthesilea are intended. For these prototypes of heroic confrontation, too, the High Classical style, especially that of Polykleitos, was appropriate.

Next comes mythology in its tragic form: bronze statues of women who probably represent the Danaids, derived from the great Danaid group in the sanctuary of Apollo on the Palatine (36–28 BC) and, like these, a mythical allegory for the struggle against Antony and Cleopatra.[35] The way in which the figures are related to Severe Style forms not only serves to underline the celebratory character of such ideology but, on top of that, leads us to the age of tragedy, in which this myth had achieved its classic form.

But other subjects called for yet other models. The bronze figures of the two wrestlers in the garden-peristyle, posed for the beginning of a bout, evoked the suggestion of real-life athletic exercise.[36] A convincing version for their active mobility could more easily be found by following Lysippos, whom Quintilian praises for having achieved an especially close approximation to *veritas*.[37] For the same reason, the Hermes sitting on the ground, with the nimble agility of his slender body, stands in the Lysippan tradition.[38]

Finally, still later Hellenistic models were adopted for the numerous figures of the Bacchic revel who populated both the *atrium* and part of the garden: satyrs, dancing, playing the flute, snapping their fingers or sleeping; then fauns and putti; also a Pan coupling with a goat; and various animals too.[39] No classicising taste, however strong, could have led to the search for fifth- and fourth-century models for these motifs. The subject decided in advance the choice of representational possibilities.

By indicating the heterogeneous models and patterns of representation of this programme of imagery, with their significance in terms of content, we have certainly not explained everything. For many of the figures in this ensemble are not, strictly speaking, copies of earlier originals, but rather adaptations of Greek works, or even new creations in the style of Greek models; here, significantly for the content-oriented, programmatic function of the figures, there is no distinction made between faithful copying and more or less fruitful new creation: the different responses stand side by side, with equal status. And in every case, from the close copies to the new creations, the style of the sculptor executing the work is recognisable. Thus the taste of early Imperial times is, in many different ways, shown to advantage in the reception of the models: the next step would therefore be to enquire into the message behind these changes of form in the style of the period. But this task goes beyond the limits of the semantic questions here under study. To stay within the field of typology and semantics, a further, final example will serve to explain the degree of subtle nuance to which this visual language could be refined.

THE RELIEFS OF THE ARA PACIS

The case of the Ara Pacis gives a particularly striking illustration of that difficulty for the understanding of the Roman recourse to Greek figural types, which arises from the fact that the models were not usually taken over in anything like a pure form. The explanation that what is really put on display here is a strong creative potential of their own on the part of the Romans, certainly establishes an important point, yet at the same time conceals a difficulty: it leaves unanswered the questions of how the use and adaptation of the models took place, and with what thinking behind them. The Ara Pacis, as an especially multi-layered monument, is a measure of how far Roman sovereignty and flexibility in the adoption of models can be made accessible to understanding.

If the great frieze with its imposing state ceremony follows the Parthenon frieze (plates 27, 29, 31; 28, 30), then this resemblance lies primarily in the overall composition and the handling of relief.[40] The type of scene, the 'Classical procession', determines the overall appearance; it conveys for the event a quality of solemnity, of the *dignitas* and *auctoritas* of the state's leading personalities and the religious establishment.

Yet the individual figures in the procession nevertheless stand very much in different traditions. While the men in togas in some ways closely resemble figure-types from the time of the Parthenon frieze, the ruler's imposing wife and the young mothers of the Imperial house are closer to the Late Classical and Hellenistic forms which emphasise the figure; the figure of Livia has rightly been placed along with the draped female figures of the late Hellenistic phase.[41] Convincing models for the women could scarcely have been found in the fifth century. Next come the *flamines* with their specifically Roman dress, for which one could not in any strict sense turn to older typological patterns, but only to reality. Thus a generally Classical type of scene was enacted with figure-types of different provenances, whose choice was once again dictated by their subjects.

These heterogeneous figure-types, however, are not placed abruptly side by side but, through the execution of detail, are assimilated to their neighbours. Certainly the toga-wearers, in accordance with their basically Classical type, also follow Classical forms fairly closely in the execution of their drapery,[42] whereas the figure of Livia shows Hellenistic features in the single, sharply pulled-in folds, enveloping her in diverging zig-zags; yet here too the stylistic phases

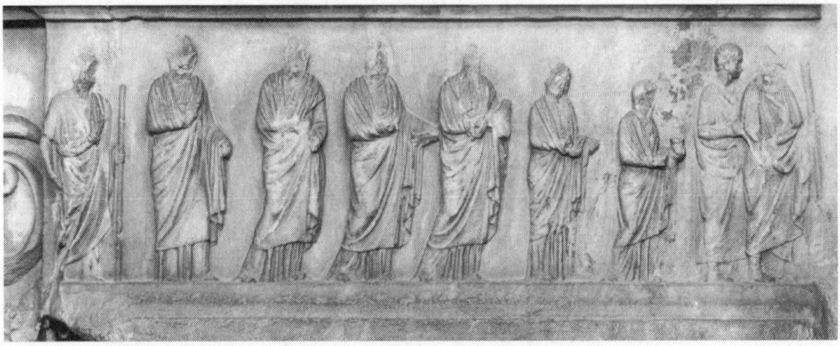

Plate 44: Ara Pacis, Small frieze

cannot be so neatly divided. The 'Classical' figure-type of Agrippa displays, in the lower part of the toga, a series of tight, sharply clashing fold-patterns that can only be traced to the Hellenistic tradition;[43] conversely, the leading female figure on the North frieze has subtly wrinkled fold-lines, which are surprisingly close to the drapery-style of the Parthenon, worked into her Hellenistic-type drapery.[44] In this sense, the different figure-types are clothed in a scarcely dissoluble mixture of Classical and Hellenistic patterns of folds. This fusion of the Classical and the Hellenistic has probably both a formal aspect and a subject-oriented one: on the one hand, the visual effect was enhanced by enriching the dignity of the Classical style with the richer contrasts of the Hellenistic. On the other, the procession as a real-life event could only be made convincingly vivid by the inclusion of a certain measure of realism – that is, of Hellenistic treatment of detail; by analogy, the figures could be furnished with individualised heads without risking any contradiction with their bodies.

Alongside this classicising style of representation, the small frieze that runs round the body of the altar attests to a second tradition for the portrayal of religious ceremonies (plate 44).[45] This distinction too has its subject-based aspects. On the great frieze, the singular historical event of the foundation-ceremony for the altar is graced, as an act of state, with the presence of the political leadership, shown, by way of an excerpt, as the most important members of the Imperial family and the representatives of the ruling class. In the small frieze, on the other

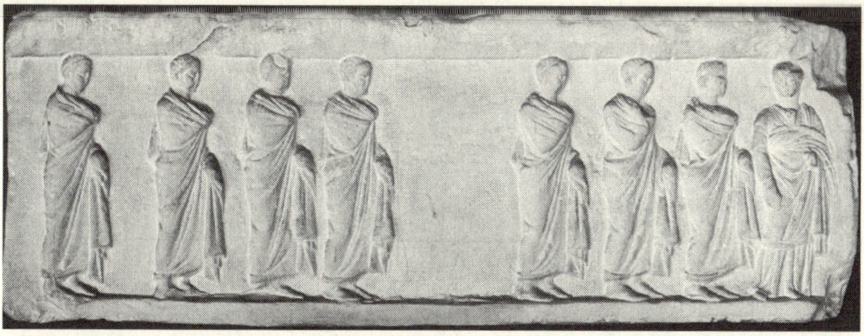

Plate 45: Detail of procession on altar-base dedicated by Atarbos, *ca.* 330–320 BC

hand, the annual religious sacrifice of this cult is evidently displayed in full ritual detail: with collective religious functionaries, who however remain cloaked in the anonymity of their office. This purpose required not the representative form of Greek High Classicism, but a type of composition that permitted the clear depiction of every detail of the sacrifice. For the 'legal' flawlessness of the sacrifice depended entirely on scrupulous observance of every detail. This demanded a paratactic form of representation, in which the individual figures can be 'counted off' through their wide spacing, largely without overlaps, often facing the viewer frontally and clearly displaying their attributes, even when this did not arise logically from the context. The origins of this style of composition are debated.[46] There are precedents not only in Hellenistic Etruria but also in Greece[47] – the Atarbos base in Athens (*ca.* 330–320 BC), for example (plate 45).[48] It seems not to be a matter of a genuinely 'Italic' phenomenon, but of an unpretentious *koine*, or common language, which was particularly widely represented in Hellenistic Italy, and which then later retained its validity for certain purposes, alongside the new and more discriminating Classical and Hellenistic forms of representation. It was a type of composition which at once lent itself to certain uses within an architectural context, above all for long-drawn-out relief friezes, whose readability could be ensured by these means. It was also particularly appropriate for subjects with a detailed enumerative character. In the small frieze of the Ara Pacis, this formal tradition achieved, through the religious precision of its subject-matter, a 'readable' kind of realism which differed

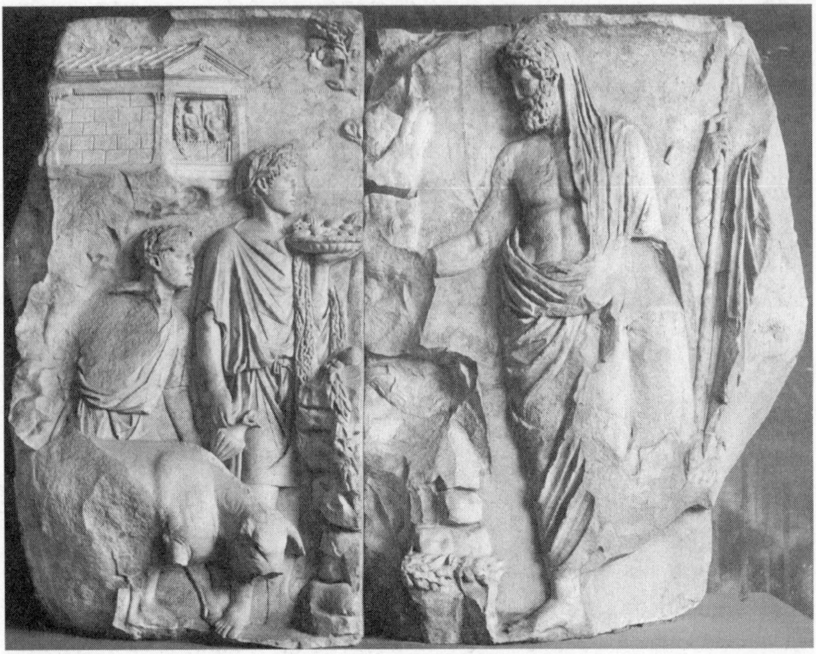

Plate 46: Ara Pacis, Aeneas relief

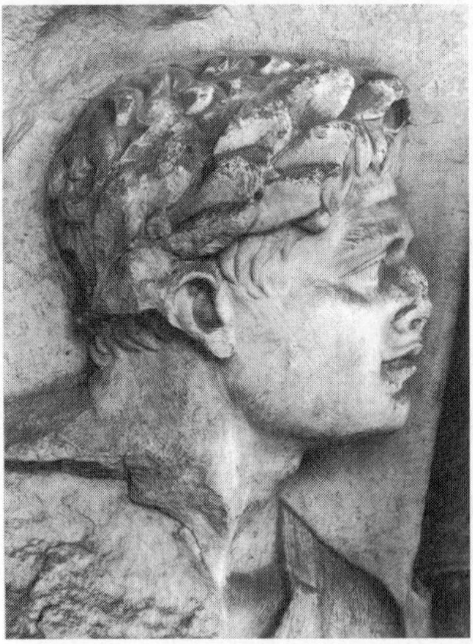

Plate 47

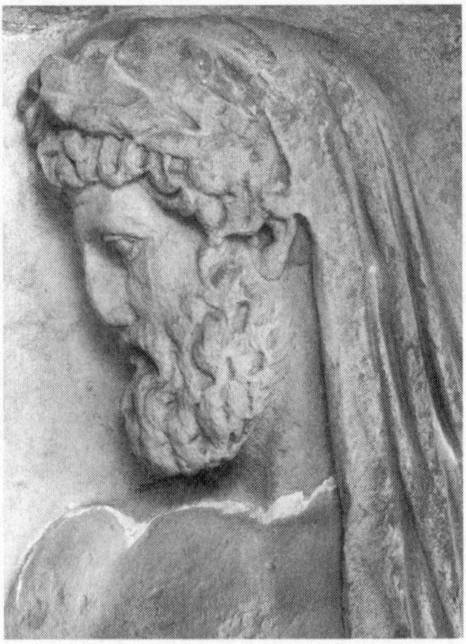

Plate 48

Plates 47–48: Ara Pacis, Aeneas relief, details

substantially from that of the thematically related but quite differently accentuated great frieze. In a similar way, the well-known examples of the Arch of Titus (after AD 81) and the Arch of Trajan at Beneventum (AD 109–14) display on their minor friezes, immediately beside the large panels with the Emperor in the centre, a triumphal procession in full paratactic detail.[49]

Other traditions again are followed in the mythological and allegorical reliefs on the faces of the entrance sides.[50] In the Aeneas relief (plate 46), a form of scene in the Hellenistic style of landscape relief is employed, because the sacrifice of the Sow of Lavinium to the Penates was to be set in an idyllic sacral landscape, for which the only convincing tradition was that derived from Hellenistic art. The figure of Aeneas on the other hand follows Classical forms, because only thus could he acquire the qualities of *auctoritas* and *pietas* necessary for his rôle of ancestor and model for the Emperor. His 'Classicism' is thus equally founded on content, as was the political bearing of Augustus in real life. Yet already the sacrificial attendants (plate 47) are distanced once again from this 'Classical' form. In particular the second figure, bending over the sow, does not merely conform, in a general way, to a basic type taken from Hellenistic sacrificial scenes; the coarse folds of the garment, too, and the head with its bulging wrinkles on the forehead and ruffled-up locks, are inconceivable without Hellenistic precedents. Here a non-Classical type is obviously being used for the lowly figure of the attendant, the more clearly to set off the solemn nobility of the Classical Aeneas (plate 48). The sow, likewise, could naturally be represented only by the realism of the Hellenistic tradition.

Yet here too the figures are shot through with formal details that cannot be explained in terms of the tradition followed for the figure in question – as where the cloak of Aeneas with its tight, steeply running folds, exhibits a Hellenistic source. A comparable method of working can be recognised, despite the severe damage in places, in the other reliefs of both the entrance-sides.

The more closely one looks into the formal design, the clearer it becomes that the employment of inherited forms took place in a finely differentiated gradation. The distinction made between type of scene, type of figure and formula for detail is thus to be understood as only a crude, preliminary classification. In reality, a rich sequence of stages, from the whole to the detail, is involved; at every stage, the entire repertoire of Greek art was available for use, to be applied in accordance with the intended message of the subject.

NOTES

1. See chapter 3 n.7.
2. The questions which here arise over the definition of 'neo-Attic' art cannot be gone into here. Cain (1985) 3, 140f., 147f. advocates to a great extent setting aside the expression 'neo-Attic'. For further arguments, see Grassinger (1991) 12. The thematic aspect here emphasised is certainly not the only, perhaps not even the predominant, element in this phenomenon; especially important too, as Grassinger shows, is the decorative purpose served by the particular object carrying the imagery. To this extent, the phenomenon can be compared with the narrative style of the 'Small Frieze' of the Ara Pacis (above, pp. 78f.).
3. Quint., *Inst.* 12.10.8.
4. Zanker (1974) 6, no. 3. That here too there are 'exceptions' – that is, different subjects – is part of the nature of the 'system'; see pp. 97–100 below.
5. Fink (1964); Zanker (1974) 77f.
6. Quint., *Inst.* 12, 10, 9.
7. Lippold (1950) 284. On what follows, see in greater detail Hölscher (1967) 122ff. and (1970) 72ff. (with earlier literature).
8. Lippold (1950) 370.
9. Coin-issues of Mallos and Herakleia Pontika: Head (1911) 724 and 515. Compare Hölscher (1967) 100.
10. Hölscher (1967) 98f.
11. Hölscher (1967) 123, 126 and (1970) 73f.
12. Hölscher (1967) 123f., pl. 11.5.
13. Hölscher (1970) 67ff., pls. 54ff.
14. L'Orange (1932); Schmidt (1968) 85–94, pls. 60ff.; Fittschen (1982) 46, no. 7; Fittschen and Zanker (1985), no. 64.
15. Lippold (1950) 186; Schuchhardt (1977) 33ff.
16. See chapter 8 n.20.
17. This point of view appears, in an opposite sense, in Lucian, *Imagines*, 6: the nude body of the Knidia is not to be employed for his Pandora.
18. On what follows, Pochmarski (1990) 513ff., esp. 525ff.; Schröder (1989). On the Classical model, Schröder (1986).

19. *Brunn/Bruckmann* pl. 652; Helbig[4] IV, no. 3297 (W. Fuchs); Willers (1975) 63. Compare pp. 103–4 below for the semantic significance of archaism.
20. Lippold (1923) 189ff.; Kraus (1959); Clairmont (1966) 21f.; Zanker (1974) 97ff. For some of these Antinoös figures, a further point of connection must have been the sharp inclination of the head of the Tiber Apollo, which helped in formulating the sentimental thoughtfulness of the youth (e.g. the Delphi statue: Clairmont (1966) 39, no. 1; Zanker (1974) 98, pl. 74.3). Other figures on the other hand (such as the Antinoös of the Banca Nazionale in Rome, Clairmont (1966) 48, no. 28; Zanker (1974) 97f., pl. 74.1) exchange this very feature for a more impressive frontality.
21. The Antinoös of the Banca Nazionale: see previous note. The Antinoös Casali in Copenhagen: Clairmont (1966) 47, no. 26.
22. Clairmont (1966) 50, no. 33. Zanker (1974), 10f., no. 9, pl. 5.4.
23. Clairmont (1966) 51, no. 38. Bartocchini (1929) 114ff. It seems that the portrait-head of Antinoös was later placed on an older statue of Apollo of the Lykeios type. This naturally does not release us from the question of the meaning of this reuse. Antinoös is characterised as Bacchus by an ivy-wreath: as with the use of the Tiber Apollo (above, n.20), it is not the mythological meaning of the model, but the general message conveyed by the body-type, that is being taken over. The bodily ideals for Apollo and for Dionysos were, in Roman times, broadly identical, as is shown by the frequent reuse of the Lykeios type for Dionysos. On this see Schröder (above, n.18). The changes are thus consistent with the semantic meaning of the type.
24. Clairmont (1966) 52f., no. 43; Zanker (1974) 99, pl. 75.1–3; Fittschen and Zanker (1985) no. 57; Gasparri (1983–4) has questioned whether the head and body originally belonged together, and explains the figure as a pastiche from a late antique workshop, which joined a damaged satyr-figure with a no longer contemporary head of Antinoös (to decorate the Baths of Diocletian?); the ears of the head would have been removed and replaced by new satyr's ears. There are several arguments against this. The head of Antinoös is turned so sharply that it must have belonged to an agitated figure, from the pine-wreath probably in the form of a dancing satyr. Its scale is, in comparison with other Antinoös heads, unusually small, more or less in accordance with that of the torso. The stylistic forms, not only of the head but also – unambiguously in my opinion – of the body too, belong to Hadrianic times. It would be an improbable coincidence for the workshop to have found, for a damaged satyr-figure, a suitable and at the same time unusually mobile and unusually small Antinoös head with the right satyr-attributes, and from the same period into the bargain, and all this after a century and a half. To this we may add that the joining surfaces are too

irregular for a secondary attachment; that, on the neck, a slender lock of hair runs over the joint with the back; and that similarly the reworking, which affected not only the ears but the neck hair as well, can also apparently be detected again beyond the joint. All this seems to point to the fact that the head and body originally belonged together, and that after Hadrian's death the head was reworked into that of a 'normal' satyr.

25. For what follows, see the overall interpretation of the sculptural decoration by Pandermalis (1971). Only when this essay was in press did the monograph of Wojcik (1986) come to my attention: it should be included in all the citations which follow (I have cited it only where there is a difference in our interpretations).
26. Pandermalis (1971) 177, 198, no. 5; Noelke (1967) 38–57, esp. 46.
27. Pandermalis (1971) 202, nos. 22 and 23 (poetess or Muse). The counterparts of these two busts are perhaps to be understood in a similar way: a replica of the Polykleitan Herakles (Pandermalis (1971) 202, no. 24) and a variant of the Lansdowne Herakles (Pandermalis (1971) 202, no. 25), which Pandermalis (1971) 180 has interpreted as a Hellenistic ruler-type. If this were correct, then once again Herakles as a divine/heroic prototype would be represented in the older style of the High Classical, but as living disciple in the more realistic forms of the fourth century. But the interpretation remains uncertain.
28. Pandermalis (1971) 183, 205, no. 41; Harrison (1965) 73ff.; Willers (1975) 60f.; Brouskari in Kyrieleis (1986) 77–83 with a new proposal for the dating of the original, on which I am unwilling to take a position without autopsy. For the questions discussed here, whether the original was an archaising work of Classical, or even late Hellenistic, date is a secondary issue.
29. On this see also Hölscher (1984b), esp. 194ff.
30. Pandermalis (1971) 183f., 205, no. 46.
31. Pandermalis (1971) 183f., 205, no. 47.
32. Pandermalis (1971) 207, no. 58; Wojcik (1986) 253ff., no. O 1 (a different view on the arrangement).
33. Pandermalis (1971) 185f., 207, no. 59 (further copy of the Polykleitan Herakles). Wojcik (1986) 71ff., no. B 15 (a different view on the arrangement).
34. Pandermalis (1971) 184f., 206, nos. 51 and 52. In any event, the female head does not belong to the type of the Mattei Amazon, compare Weber (1978) and (1984), esp. 108ff.
35. Pandermalis (1971) 181f., 203f., nos. 32–36; Rumpf (1950); Diehl (1964) 145f.; Sgobbo (1971) [1972]; Trillmich (1973), esp. 256ff.; Zanker (1983), esp. 27ff.; Schneider (1986) 79f.; Simon (1986) 21ff.
36. Pandermalis (1971) 181, 203, no. 31.

37. See above, n.6.
38. Pandermalis (1971) 179, 200f., no. 18; Beschi (1962) 47f., with the demonstration that the Hermes represents a classicising adaptation of an older type, in mirror-image.
39. Pandermalis (1971) 201, nos. 19, 20, 21; 202, nos. 26 and 27; 208, nos. 62, 63, 64.
40. Above, pp. 49ff.
41. Horn (1931) 87.
42. Chapter 6 n.11.
43. Simon (1967) pl. 14. Compare above, p. 16, on the Aeneas of the Ara Pacis.
44. Compare Simon (1967), pl. 16 upper with Brommer (1977), pl. 185 lower; Borbein (1975) figs. 3 and 4.
45. Simon (1967) 15, pl. 9; Rodenwaldt (1940) 12–43, esp. 40f.; Felletti Maj (1977) 275ff.
46. On this, see Rodenwaldt (1940) 12ff.; Bianchi Bandinelli (1967); Felletti Maj (1977) *passim*; Hölscher (1981); Brandenburg (1979) and (1981); Pfanner (1983) 84f.; Settis (1982) 171ff. I do not wish here to go into the various alternative explanations of the origins of this style – which undoubtedly incorporate some of the truth – but merely to show to best advantage its thematic aspects.
47. Pfanner (1983) 85.
48. Casson (1921) 240ff., no. 1338. Compare too Svoronos (1937) pl. cci.
49. On the Arch of Titus, the same episode appears twice, with different emphases, which is basically comparable with the two – admittedly different – religious processions of the Ara Pacis.
50. Above, pp. 16–18.

CHAPTER 8

The semantic system: premisses and structure

If one takes together the elements outlined here, then the outcome is that, in late Hellenistic and Roman times, the stylistic forms of the different epochs of Greek art were taken up for one reason in particular: because in this way different subjects and themes, each in its specific form, could be most aptly represented. The concept of eclecticism is not erroneous, but it only imprecisely describes the facts of the case: it is not an arbitrary relativism that prevails, nor a pure preference of taste, but a selection, which is geared towards best expressing the message. For each subject – to be precise, for each thematic aspect within a subject – there were established patterns available, which were of diachronically different origins, but now became synchronically applicable side by side. Thus there arose a system in which the forms of Greek art were filtered, not according to stylistic criteria but primarily according to semantic ones, and could thus now be used with an entirely new meaning. In this sense, one can speak of a semanticisation of the styles.

GENERAL PREMISSES

The precondition for this was to be found in the overall basic principles of earlier Greek and of late Hellenistic and Roman art respectively. The essential feature of this phenomenon consists in the fact that structures of form which had once, in the course of Greek history, been fundamental expressions of entire epochs, now acquired a new function as part of a system with an entirely different basis. In the centuries from the Archaic to the Hellenistic periods, Greek art had gone through a rapid and radical process of change, deeply stamped with the collective experiences of the successive epochs, and corresponding to the comprehensive historical development from the Homeric chiefdoms to the Hellenistic *oikoumenē*. In this process, different forms of representation were certainly devised, contemporaneously, for different subjects; but overall, the decisive element was a strong developmental dynamic, which characterised the full range of forms of each individual period. The unity of the various products of a given epoch thus predominated relatively strongly, as against the continuity of particular themes across the boundaries of periods.

During these earlier phases of Greek culture the realisation, in artistic form, of historical conditions rested on a very concrete experience of life and of the world. The premisses and the particular nature of this phenomenon cannot be adequately described within the framework of this study. But the outcome is clear: the fundamental philosophy of human reality, because of its concreteness, found visible expression in the forms of figural art in a very direct way: the relation of man to his environment in the concept of space, the idea of human interactions in the group compositions, the conception of the organic function of the body in the way that the human figure was constructed, the interest in material reality and its appearance in the fashioning of surfaces. Thus, notwithstanding the marked changes in the idea of man and his world from epoch to epoch, a fundamental premiss long remained in force: the starting assumption, down to the second century BC, was that the essential aspects of the world could be grasped as concrete, physical reality; every change in the range of possible artistic forms can thus be understood as being, at the same time, a further gain in terms of new reality.

In contrast with this, the new system of visual language, which was shaped in late Hellenistic times and remained in operation throughout the Roman Imperial period, represents not merely a new phase of development, but a fundamental break.

On the one hand, the tasks of artistic imagery were essentially no longer handled by developing new forms of representation, but by having recourse to a diversity of older traditions. These formal resources, which in the past had been developed one after the other, were now available for use together. Out of a diachronic development, there came into being a synchronic range.

At the same time, the co-existence of a variety of forms of representation signified a fundamental departure from the apprehension of reality which had hitherto been so forcefully pushed ahead. In terms of realism, the formal means available from the different periods was altogether diverse. Certainly, realistic approaches to representation enjoyed a further lease of life, and were indeed still further refined, to produce the well-known types of realism in Roman art. But from now on they remained confined to specific fields of the figural arts, and appeared alongside many other forms of representation.[1] A unified vision of reality was no longer achievable.

THE ABSTRACTION OF CONTENT AND THE STANDARDISATION OF FORM

The basis for this lies in a far-reaching change: visible reality came to be seen, more and more, as signifying abstract ideas. In the art theory of the time, this tendency took the form of the development of a system of abstract expressions for artistic effects.[2] The influences on the iconographic phenomena are obvious; they are at their clearest in monuments whose subject-matter is political.[3]

There is a series of sarcophagi of Roman military commanders, displaying a sequence of episodes from the careers of the leading military class;[4] the order in which they are arranged is striking from a chronological point of view: first a battle, then the ensuing subjugation and pardoning of the enemy, only then the (actually preceding) sacrifice on departure before the outbreak of war, and finally the marriage ceremony which had usually taken place at an earlier stage still. The arrangement of the scenes is not to be taken as a factual, biographical sequence, but as a systematic conception of ideal values, of the primary political virtues: *virtus*, *clementia*, *pietas* and *concordia*.

The representation of state triumphs was similarly handled. A series of reliefs from a triumphal arch of Marcus Aurelius (after AD 176) shows twelve selected scenes from the wars against the

Marcomanni,[5] in which not the decisive turning-points of the fighting, but representative ceremonial events and measures are displayed, in which the Emperor embodies a canon of exemplary political models: here too the subjugation-scene stands as exemplar for *clementia*, the sacrifice as an instance of *pietas*, the departure and the triumphal procession alike as signs of *virtus*.

Together, these virtues compose a kind of ideological system which had been developed under the late Republic, which certainly underwent certain modifications in the course of the Imperial period, but which in principle retained a more or less static validity for centuries on end and, as such, was assigned to the individual emperors and leading men of Rome to fulfil. In this sense, Roman state art as a whole served not simply to record historical reality, but much more to exemplify intellectual ideals. The term *exemplum* conveys well that combination of conferment of meaning, stereotyping, abstraction and resistance to change which characterises this phenomenon.[6]

The forms of representation in figural art are affected, in an informative way, by these premisses. If historical events were above all to exemplify general models of political and social conduct, then the consistent portrayal of reality played only a secondary rôle. A scene from Trajan's Column, which shows the building of a fortification by the Roman army in the presence of the Emperor, serves to bring this out.[7] The soldiers' work was meant to illustrate the energetic surmounting of manifold obstacles and toil, the ruler's countenance to represent the presence of authority. Thus the laborious building activities could best unfold within the spatial depth of the Hellenistic tradition: while on the other hand the authority of the ruler, with his entourage, could be more convincingly represented by the use of parallel, frontal figures. Two concepts of space, difficult to reconcile from the point of view of recording reality, here clash with one another: the group round the Emperor gives the impression of a curiously abrupt insertion. In keeping with this is the fact that the scene is scarcely imaginable as a coherent event in reality either: the Emperor had no practical function in the building of the fortification, so that the other scenes with this subject, almost without exception, manage perfectly well without him; and if the meaning were really that he was physically inspecting the work, then the soldiers would have to be paying more attention to him. The Emperor's presence has in fact more of an ideal quality: this achievement of the Roman army, too, is to appear as being placed under his direction. From such an ideological viewpoint, the coherence of reality was less important than the immediate intelligibility of the intellectual meaning: *labor* for the soldiers, *maiestas* for the ruler.

The tendency to reduce historical reality – and this goes for other areas of reality as well – to imagined abstractions opened the way to stylisation of the most varied kind. One aspect of this phenomenon is the borrowing of Classical forms, from the second century BC onwards, side by side with the continuation of Hellenistic traditions. In addition, this process undoubtedly demanded that the method of representation be set in a durable typology.

The sacrificial scenes on the sarcophagi closely reproduce a type of composition which, though preserved in fragmentary form, is already present on a major state monument of Claudian date.[8] The type here signifies, not the placatory sacrifice to Jupiter by a military commander setting out, but a solemn state sacrifice to Mars Ultor, unquestionably with the Emperor at its centre. Further examples of this type are shown in yet other scenes of sacrifice.[9] Here, then, quite different historical events are brought to expression in the same formula of imagery. This phenomenon has two sides to it. In the first place, the specific historical reality of the various events was destined to become unimportant, if they were seen only from the point of view of exemplifying *pietas*: from this angle, the correctness of the ritual enactment alone was important, in that it was in fact always observed and reproduced with precision, but not the distinctiveness of each event. Secondly, the artistic composition likewise no longer received any important stimulus from such an abstract view of events: the organic construction of the body and its potential for action in space – that is, the basis on which Greek art had comprehended reality – were entirely insignificant for the exemplification of *pietas* and other virtues, and thus became secondary considerations. Certainly, neither of these things means that ideological assumptions come to stand in necessary conflict with a realistic grasp of the figures and events. What was to be demonstrated was actually that the ideal values had been transformed into reality – but they did not insist on a particularly specific and realistic style of rendering.[10]

Much the same is true of the subjects for sculpture in the round. The figures of deities, personifications and heroes stood more and more for an ideal message, often abbreviated to a slogan-like form. Accordingly, the interest in 'individual' representation waned and the repertoire was progressively reduced to a stock of common types.

From such abstractness in the iconographic subject-matter, there thus arose a wide range of freedom in the borrowing of proven types and traditions. Where the recording of specific reality was no longer a pressing aim, images of different epochs and with different views of reality could be put to use side by side. For the more abstract themes, one needed formulae which derived their power to convince, not from a specific reality, but from their effect in ideal terms. For the range of religious sacrifices which were understood as representing the same virtue of *pietas*, the use of a stereotyped formula of imagery suggested itself, to say the least, and that for centuries on end. The imagery adopted, which had at one time occupied a specific place in the diachronic development of Greek art, was thereby tied to subject-specific messages and transferred to the much more static field of typology. It is similar to the linguistic process by which formerly stylistic phenomena, belonging to specific periods or groups, are transformed into stylistically neutral, isolated elements of vocabulary, of set phrases or of syntax.

Realistic elements were certainly not expelled from art in the process. On the contrary, Roman art was frequently fixated, to the highest degree, on realistic effects and the deceptive glossing over of the boundary between art and nature.[11] But these forms of realism, too, are subordinated to the semantic system. The much-invoked 'realism' of Roman art is not a general style which prevailed over all artistic production; it is a very partial realism, which was adopted for specific themes and messages: for energy and exertion, age, suffering and death, sensual charm, animals and landscape; in other ways, for political and social attributes; and, at certain periods, especially for the portrait.[12] All in all, a limited sample of the whole range of production, and one determined from the standpoints of theme and content.

The language of imagery that arose in this way was a rich system of visual communication which provided either fixed formulae, or easily applied patterns of formulation, for every possible theme or subject. The relatively static formal methods corresponded to the relative constancy of the content of ideas.

THE STRUCTURE OF THE SEMANTIC SYSTEM

How could this visual language achieve its validity throughout the entire Empire, with its very diverse population-groups? On what intellectual premisses did it rest? What was its intellectual standing? How was it possible for this language of imagery, assuming that it has been more or less accurately described, on the one hand to take effect in ways that were both highly ambitious and dependent on many presuppositions; on the other, to be a mass-phenomenon of the whole Empire? In fact this peculiarity of being, at the same time, part of the cultural heritage of the élite and common visual language for the broad population of the Empire, is easily intelligible on the basis of the formal system that has been outlined.

The decisive point is that, in this system, specific types of imagery were not mechanically tied to individual subjects for representation. Rather, the inherited types of image and style represented, in the first instance, a system of expressive values, and these values were decisive for the linkage between form and subject. Yet this system, whose forms were, at one and the same time, values, was accessible both to theoretical reflection and to spontaneous artistic practice.[13]

a. Theoretical views of art

On one side, the system has theoretical underpinnings. According to the dominant classicising theory of art, the assessment and reception of the different Greek art-styles was not simply based on the direct impression made by individual exemplary masterpieces, but additionally and especially on a range of general values, which tied the realm of visible forms to that of *ēthos*; a phenomenon which has to do with the more abstract understanding of art from late Hellenistic times onwards.[14]

The art of Pheidias was praised for its sublime and revered grandeur: *semnotēs* and *megethos* are named again and again as distinctive qualities.[15] They are accompanied by supreme beauty, *kallos*, *eximia pulchritudo*.[16] These are qualities appropriate for the representation of the highest essence of divinity. *Kallos* and *megethos* are at issue when Dio Chrysostom asks whether Pheidias, in his Zeus at Olympia (*ca.* 430 BC), had represented 'the fitting form and appropriate shape of the god's nature' (*to prepon eidos kai tēn axian morphēn tēs theou phuseōs*).[17] And this appropriateness of the form as an expression of divinity is further differentiated: 'the strength and magnificence of the form' (*to ischuron tou eidous kai to megaloprepes*) displays his royal power, 'the qualities of gentleness and kind affection' (*to praion kai prosphiles*) his fatherly care, 'the dignity and severity' (*hē te semnotēs kai to austēron*) his protection of the community and laws of the *polis*, and so on.[18] For Quintilian, similarly, *pondus*, *maiestas* and *pulchritudo* are the expressive values whereby Pheidias, above all others, brought the essence and the *auctoritas* of the gods to their highest level of representation, indeed added something further to the traditional veneration of the gods:[19] the artist as theologian. According to Quintilian, these same qualities, if at a slightly lower level, also distinguished the cult-statues of Alkamenes.[20]

Polykleitos on the other hand did not, according to Quintilian, endow the gods so impressively with *pondus* and *auctoritas*, but instead excelled all other sculptors in his *decor* and *diligentia*. It was above all to the human figure, and exclusively to its youthful form, that he was said to have lent *decor supra verum*.[21] Accordingly Quintilian describes Polykleitos' ideal body, that of the Doryphoros, as 'fit as well for military service as for the exercise ground' (*aptum vel militiae vel palaestrae*), and places it among 'the bodies of other young men engaged in warfare or athletics' (*aliorum iuvenum bellicosorum et athletarum corpora*).[22] On these values of artistic expression, Polykleitos' fame for the portrayal of youthful heroes and athletes in Classical *kalokagathia* is founded.

With Kallimachos, in turn, it was his *leptotes*, *charis*, *elegantia* that were admired.[23] In his most famous work, the 'Spartan Dancing Women' (late fifth century BC) (*saltantes Lacaenae*), it is clearly the delicately waving movements of the 'Rich Style' that are meant here; they are qualities that could above all become patterns for dancing and hovering figures.

With Lysippos and Praxiteles, finally, Quintilian praises them for having 'most satisfactorily come close to reality' (*ad veritatem accessisse optime*).[24] This quality of realism, which is frequently emphasised in both their cases, must once again have commended itself for certain specific subjects. Lysippos was famed among other things for his portraits, and there is repeated emphasis on their 'closest resemblance' (*summa similitudo*).[25] In his portrayal of Alexander the Great (*ca.* 330 BC), especially, he convincingly represented, in Plutarch's words, the *arete*, more precisely 'the manliness and lion-like quality' (*to arrenopon kai leontōdes*); in Horace's, the 'face of the courageous Alexander' (*fortis Alexandri vultum*).[26] Lysippos' modelling of the head evidently stood for dynamic emotional power. His bodies on the other hand are said to have been 'rather slender but healthy' (*graciliora siccioraque*), and their 'elongation' (*proceritas*) is emphasised.[27] All of these are qualities which make it understandable that Lysippos later acquired great importance above all for his representation of active athletes, and of their protagonists Herakles and Hermes.

Praxiteles on the other hand is celebrated again and again for the soft, thoroughly concrete seductiveness of his body-surfaces, and for the soulful expressions of his faces.[28] These are qualities of especial validity for figures of youthful, sensual appearance. It was indeed his figures of Aphrodite and her devotees which, in later documentary sources as in later imagery, found the greatest resonance;[29] but the same soft sensuality was also to be attributed by Kallistratos to a Dionysos by Praxiteles.[30] It was these qualities which, for instance, then recommended the 'Praxitelean' Apollo Lykeios type as a model for figures of Dionysos or Bacchus.

To these may be added stylistic forms which play little or no rôle in the classicising literature of art, but whose general importance can be recognised from the works themselves: those of the Archaic period as a mark of venerable tradition;[31] those of the Hellenistic age as an expression of dynamic pathos and laborious effort, or indeed of an idyllic atmosphere.

On occasion, several periods could even provide patterns for the same group of subjects, and this without fundamental differences in meaning. Animal figures were the glory of the Severe Style, of Myron and Kalamis – but also of Lysippos.[32] The pronounced realism found in the most famous examples was acclaimed. Lysippos here, as often, stands as forerunner of Hellenistic art, and his animal representations were in practice much imitated. To some extent, he functioned as the last representative of Classicism, and his good reputation justified many a form which could otherwise easily have fallen victim to the verdict of an 'age of decline'.[33] The affinity between the early Hellenistic and Severe Styles, in their tendency to realism, is thus already made plain in the ancient reception of both periods.[34]

Finally, the specific characterisation of the individual qualities of style (*aretai*, *virtutes*) of the various masters also makes possible comparisons between them. Quintilian contrasted the individual artists in terms of these qualities.[35] In a similar way, Dionysios of Halikarnassos names Kalamis and Kallimachos as being more gifted for lesser and for human themes, on account of their *leptotēs* and *charis*; Pheidias and Polykleitos, on the other hand, because of their mastery of the 'solemn' (*semnon*), the 'sublime' (*megalotechnon*) and the 'dignified' (*axiōmatikon*), as more successful for greater and for divine subjects.[36] Conversely, Fronto considers that it would be absurd to demand playful subjects of Pheidias, or statues of gods and the like of Kalamis.[37] Each artist has his own specific qualities, and is thus particularly suited to specific themes. In combination, the various artists make up a broad, more or less complete spectrum of possibilities for expression, as also of subject.

Through the use of these values of expression, which form the basis for the cultivated judgment of art, the inherited forms were made available for Roman purposes. This undoubtedly involved a reinterpretation of the original intentions behind these forms: one that is already shown in the fact that the various forms originally arose from the experiences of whole epochs, so covering a wide range of artistic subjects, and in succession to one another; whereas they were now made available for simultaneous use, disregarding the boundaries of the historical periods, each for its specific subject. It was only when taken together, as a 'system', that the various forms more or less covered the spectrum of intended meanings.

But even though the different forms of representation belonged, side by side, to the same system of visual language, they nevertheless stood in a hierarchical relationship to one another. For the values of expression to which the forms were linked had different rankings. Of the terms which stood under generally classicising auspices, *maiestas* and *pondus* had a higher rating than emotional dynamic. This had the result, in Augustan times for example, that Classical traditions of form were taken over above all for subjects that had especially high prestige: such as for the most important deities and for state events – and among the latter, for solemn ceremonies rather than for battles. Lesser, and hostile, figures on the other hand could stay more with the Hellenistic tradition: such as barbarians, giants or satyrs.

From the hierarchy of values, there developed a hierarchy of forms, with dominant elements at the centre and adjunct elements of lesser importance. If, as in Flavian times, the hierarchy of values underwent a partial change, then a corresponding change in the relation of the forms could also happen. But even then, the fundamental association of forms, values and subjects remained in force.

A decisive consequence of this system is that the different stylistic forms, which had made their appearance in Greek art diachronically, were to some extent de-historicised in the new system of themes and values of expression. Concepts like *maiestas*, *gratia*, *veritas* acquire a meaning not as a historical sequence, but only as a synchronic system; just as do the subjects for representation – gods, heroes, athletes, animals.

This system of ideal values, which in Hellenistic and Roman times were associated – both for learned students of art and for the educated public – with the various stylistic forms in the history of Greek art, requires yet more detailed investigation based on the written sources. But the consequences for their employment can be clearly seen in the works of art themselves.

The fundamental fact is that these values of artistic appreciation are clearly elevated from the sphere of sensual impressions into that of ethical models. A level of intellectual abstraction was thereby achieved, comparable with that in the relationship between reality and history, whose events were likewise understood as realisations of general ethical models of conduct. And the concepts which governed the process in these two spheres are very closely connected – indeed, in part identical, as with *dignitas* or *maiestas*. These ideational values are at the very interface between subject and form. To express it in a very simplistic way:

SUBJECTS	VALUES	FORMS [of]
Gods	*maiestas, pondus, eximia pulchritudo*	Pheidias
Heroes	*decor supra verum*	Polykleitos
Human figures	*veritas, pulchritudo*	Lysippos, Praxiteles
Animals, satyrs, giants	*veritas*	Severe Style, Lysippos, Hellenistic

Thus it was only because of their generalised ideational meaning that the diverse forms of representation became suitable for the formulation of the subjects of Roman imagery: Pheidian frieze-composition suggested itself for dignified state ceremonies above all for its *maiestas*, Hellenistic mass movement for battles because of its emotional dynamic.

But if ideal values acted as the link between the subjects and the forms of imagery, then this is one reason why not a rigid code of rules, but a flexible system came into being.

On the one hand the subjects, in their ideational meanings, were not absolutely fixed from the outset, but allowed a certain latitude in interpretation: Bacchus could be conceived in his time-honoured dignity, or as a manifestation of youthful sensuality; and the choice of forms could be made in a correspondingly diverse way – archaising in the former case, Praxitelean in the latter. The theme suggested specific forms of representation, but it did not wholly determine the form. It left open a choice between more or less plausible stylistic forms which, for their part, then interpreted the theme from this or from that aspect: for Bacchus, even a representation in the noble dignity of the High Classical, or in the conqueror's dynamism of the Hellenistic, is not wholly excluded. On the other hand, the various modes of representation and figural types were, equally, not altogether rigidly fixed in their ideal message. By comparison with the original meanings of the forms in Greek art, transplanting them to the new ideal context of Roman culture already represented a change; and further shifts of meaning from then on were not excluded. It is certainly an extreme instance when, in the case of Kallimachos, there was not even unanimity as to whether his figures were distinguished by their *gratia*, or whether they lacked precisely this quality;[38] but even with Pheidias, the united chorus of commendation displays a certain spectrum, from *kallos* and *pulchritudo*, *phōs* and *charis*, to *megethos* and *semnotēs*.[39]

So the system of subjects, ideational values and forms of imagery allowed, at both its points of linkage, a certain degree of freedom for interpretation and artistic taste. And this flexibility was also preserved through the fact that no theoretician apparently ever undertook the task of bringing together these concepts into a consistent schema and then presenting it as binding. It was rather a conglomeration of artistic judgments which, in the end, were so complementary to each other that it acquired a certain systematic character.

The flexible structure of this system made it possible for a given subject not always to appear in the same form of representation. On the other hand, neither is the range of variation so broad as to prevent the increasing acceptance of certain judgments. And in this flexibility, too, the semantic significance of the form remains manifest.[40]

b. Sculptural practice

Roman sculptors were certainly as a rule not theoreticians, but manual workers, who did not think about aesthetic value-systems; the same was true of the general public. But what the writers on art had formulated in theory could have, indeed must have, resulted in unpremeditated, spontaneous practice. The commissioning of a statue, it goes without saying, affected the subject in the first instance. The sculptor, seeking a suitable model for it, could doubtless perceive by pure intuition which models from Greek art were, according to the popular ways of thinking in his time, the most appropriate ones. A venerable idol must be executed not in the Hellenistic, but in the Archaic style; Bacchus as a figure of sensuality not in the early Classical, but in the Praxitelean; a satyr not in the Pheidian, but in the Hellenistic – not on grounds of theoretical reflection, but simply because it made sense to him. Anyone who wanted a theoretical basis for this could then find it in the concepts of the writers on art.

The understanding of the viewer must have operated in a similarly unthinking way. In so far as he paid any attention, not just to the factual content but to the form as well, its messages were very general impressions like *maiestas* or *pathos*, which could be transmitted more or less directly, without any apparatus of theory.

Reflection, less on the style than on the content, may in many cases have played a rôle as well: with the Aphrodite of Capua type, for instance, on the exposure of the body or the position of the arms. To this may certainly be added external circumstances, in a variety of forms: Greek images in famous locations, such as Athens or Rome, were predestined to play a bigger part as models than those to which the Roman art industry had less easy access;[41] and in individual cases, the repertoire of models available to the various workshops will have depended on many chance factors. A final factor must have been the location of display, the scale and perhaps the context of other pre-existing works, planned for the image; not least, how much the client was prepared to pay.

A variety of stimuli and imponderables thus determined the language of imagery in the practice of the sculptors' workshops. But among these, a specially important rôle was clearly played by the usefulness of certain styles and figural types for each specific subject. Admittedly, in sculptural practice too, the link between subject and imagery was neither fixed nor consistent. It was a repertory, gradually evolved, of inherited forms and potential formulae; the choice between them remained ultimately a matter of taste – one which brought about a certain collective coherence, but which admitted of divergence.

The interrelation between the two attitudes, the theoretical and the spontaneous, is obvious. Both contributed, not to the forming and preserving of a strict classification, but to establishing a certain set of rules for practice, whereby appropriate modes of representation and figural types were found for various subjects and messages. These rules then tended to acquire, in a fairly short time, a certain coherence and consistency. In this general sense, we can reasonably speak of a system.

NOTES

1. Above, p. 91 and below, pp. 116–17.
2. Above, p. 92 and below, n.14.
3. Summarised in Hölscher (1980a), from which I repeat as little as possible. The conclusions reached here for the language of imagery form a companion-piece to the reflections developed there (pp. 317ff.) on the thematics of representational art.
4. Rodenwaldt (1935) 3ff.; Hölscher (1980a) 288ff.; Koch and Sichtermann (1982) 99. For an important recent contribution, Reinsburg (1984).
5. Scott Ryberg (1967).
6. Kornhardt (1936).
7. Cichorius (1896–1900), pl. 12; Lehmann-Hartleben (1926) pl. 9, xi/xii; Hölscher (1980a) 321; compare 294f.
8. Cagiano de Azavedo (1951) 56ff., no. 47, pl. x.1; Scott Ryberg (1955) 69ff., fig. 36d; Torelli (1982) 70ff. On the type in general: Brendel (1930). For what follows, compare Hölscher (1980a) 317ff.
9. Brendel (1930) *passim*.
10. Thus in art, as in the grasp of historical reality, it was hardly a matter of conscious abstraction; rather, there arose, in the guise of an ideal plan, an increasing indifference to specific reality.
11. On this, see especially Oltramare (1941).
12. On this, see below, pp. 116f.
13. See also Zanker in *Classicisme*, 293ff.
14. On what follows, see also Robert (1886) 52f.; Schweitzer (1932) 32ff. Both point out the fact that conceptual abstraction characterises the late Hellenistic, classicising art theory, as against that of Xenokrates in early Hellenistic times. See too Jucker (1950) 132f. Only in Preisshofen and Zanker (1970–1), esp. 103f., was the phenomenon brought down to the decisive point that here a 'horizontal', that is an ahistorical, system of values is being superimposed on a 'vertical', diachronic one. The ancient sources cited here can almost all be found in Overbeck (1868). Preisshofen and Zanker (1970–1) 118, n.54 remains valid.
15. *semnotēs*: Dio Chrys., *Or.* 12.49; 12.74. On the expression, Pollitt (1974) 233ff. *megethos*: Plut., *Sull.*, 17. Demetr., *Eloc.*, 14 (*megaleion*). Plin., *HN* 36.19 (*magnificentia*); Pollitt (1974) 196ff., 198ff., 400f. Compare Dion. Hal., *Isoc.* 3 (together with Polykleitos): 'the solemn, the sublime and the

dignified' (*to semnon kai megalotechnon and axiōmatikon*) (Lat. *auctoritas*); Pollitt (1974) 139f.

16. Cicero, *Orat.*, 9; Plin., *HN* 34.54; 36.15; 36.18; Plut., *Sull.*, 17; Dio Chrys., *Or.* 12.25; 12.49; Pollitt (1974) 191ff., 423ff.
17. Dio Chrys., *Or.* 12.52. Compare 12.59 on Homer: 'He, excelling above all in beauty and dignity and magnificence' (*ho de pleiston huperbalōn kallei kai semnotēti kai megaloprepeiai*); Pollitt (1974) 217ff.
18. Dio Chrys., *Or.* 12.75–7.
19. Quint., *Inst.* 12.10.9; Pollitt (1974) 401f., 422f.
20. Quint., *Inst.* 12.10.9.
21. Quint., *Inst.* 12.10.7f. Similarly Strabo 8.6.10; Pollitt (1974) 200, 235, 422f. On *decor* and *diligentia*, Pollitt (1974) 341ff., 351ff.
22. Quint., *Inst.* 5.12.21.
23. Dion. Hal., *Isoc.* 3 (so too for Kalamis, but I prefer to spare the reader this long-running problem). Contrariwise Plin., *HN* 34.92, for whom his excessive *diligentia* prevented all *gratia* – quite intelligibly in both cases. The example shows how heavily the evaluation of the forms could also depend on subjective judgment (compare above, pp. 97–98). Pollitt (1974) 194ff., 297ff., 362ff., 380f.
24. Quint., *Inst.* 12.10.9; Moreno (1973) 159ff. Pollitt (1974) 125ff.
25. See especially, for the portraits of the *Turma Alexandri*: Plin., *HN* 34.64. Vell. Pat. 1, 11.4; Pollitt (1974) 430ff.
26. Plut., *De Alex.fort.*, 2.2; Hor., *Epist.* 2.1.240f.
27. Plin., *HN* 34.65.
28. As is well known, the sources are prolific, and relate above all to the Knidian Aphrodite: Overbeck, *Schriftquellen*, 1227–45. On the soulfulness, see too the summary verdict in the fragment Diod. Sic. 26.1.1.
29. Aphrodite: Overbeck, *Schriftquellen*, 1227ff. Eros, ibid., 1249ff. Phryne: ibid., 1269ff.
30. Kallistratos, *Stat.descr.* 8. Overbeck, *Schriftquellen*, 1222.
31. On this compare Pollitt (1974) 154ff., 449.
32. Overbeck, *Schriftquellen*, 524–7 (Kalamis); 550–92 (Myron); 1460, 1490–1, 1503–5 (Lysippos).
33. Comparable is the rôle of Demosthenes in rhetorical theory, see chapter 11 n.9 below.
34. For links between the Severe Style and early Hellenistic in the figural arts: Himmelmann (1975) 17ff., (1980) 83 and (1983) 87ff.
35. Quint., *Inst.* 12.10.3ff.
36. Dion. Hal., *Isoc.* 3.
37. Fronto, *Ad Verum imp.*, 1.1.
38. Above, n.23.
39. Above, nn.15–19.

40. For anyone who tied the ranking of styles with the ranking of political epochs, there could arise a problem, to which A. Dihle drew my attention: 'There was a difficulty here for the Romans of the Imperial period, since politically and morally, the yardstick for any Roman "classicism" had to be the third century BC, but aesthetically, the Ciceronian–Augustan period. For the Greeks, on the other hand, the fifth and fourth century BC combined both, as Dionysios of Halikarnassos, for example, expressly says. Since antiquity as a whole could rely, much more strongly than we, on the availability of the means of expression, it is understandable if the Romans showed themselves the more distinctly eclectic of the two. Thus Sallust already endorses, on moral and pedagogic grounds, the style of Cato the Elder, whose speeches Cicero describes as *horridulae*; and the question of how to judge this relationship between morality and stylistic preference is never settled (compare Sen., *Ep.* 114).'
41. The observation by Lippold (1923) 69, that there are as yet no demonstrable Roman copies even of works in Delphi and Olympia (apart from the accessories of Pheidias' Zeus), remains valid to this day.

CHAPTER 9

The origins of the system: dynamics and statics

The beginnings of this way of dealing in inherited forms lead us back into Greek art. Greek art, too, evolved specific forms for individual functions and subjects – portraits, for example, or the portrayal of socially marginal groups, or votive reliefs – which were not valid for the whole range of artistic production.[1] Yet even these special forms are almost invariably determined by a strong dynamic of development in terms of temporal style, which led to fundamental changes over the succession of epochs.

More important for the later language of imagery is the fact that from Classical times on there existed, alongside the mainstream of art that was generally 'in keeping with the period', a slender tradition of archaising forms.[2] Their use was governed by considerations which were not of a general kind relating to the style of the period, but were specifically subject-based: they were developed for statues of deities, in the context of divine cult and myth. This practice differs from the later semantic system above all in the fact that the archaistic form was no more than an anomalous deviation from the contemporary language of imagery of its period, not one of its normal elements; that the contrast between 'old-fashioned' and 'present-day' was thus highlighted; so that, in respect of their message, there were not two purely content-based positions on an equal footing, but a strong temporal dimension was retained. In this fundamental break with a unified developmental history, the dominant rôle of historical change is still clear.

In the later language of imagery, the simple antithesis between archaising and contemporary forms was, in the first place, fundamentally widened so that the whole range of forms from the Late Archaic to the late Hellenistic became available. Only then did a complex system of forms come into being. But the various forms were above all employed, not so much to express the historically 'old' and 'contemporary', but to indicate a field of meaning that tended towards atemporality and the conceptualisation of theme.[3]

The preconditions and beginnings of this language of imagery are to be sought not in Rome, but in Greek art of the second century BC. The late Hellenistic period saw a fundamental change in the relation between styles in which, simultaneously, Hellenistic stylistic forms were continued to the point of exaggeration, and Classical traditions were taken up again. A fundamentally wider range of available stylistic possibilities was thereby created. A further consequence was the overall change in the significance of the phenomenon of style: 'style' was now no longer a general, more or less self-explanatory language of expression, but was subordinated to a continuous process of selection and reflection. As to the stimuli and historical context for this process, we are still largely in the dark; nothing on these matters can be said here. The one thing that is clear is that these developments took place, in the first instance, in Greece and under Greek preconditions; and that, from the second century BC onwards, Rome took part in this Greek process. Then, however, the phenomena were developed into a much more rigorous form, and to more far-reaching effect, in Rome and for the circumstances of the Roman Empire; and in this setting they came to fulfil a specific function.[4]

In Greece, likewise, from the beginning of retrospective tendencies in the second century BC, the recourse to older models took place under thematic auspices. Damophon of Messene brought a clear element of differentiation to the group of cult-statues for the sanctuary at Lykosura (*ca.* 200–150 BC): for the dignity of Demeter, he based the head on a Classical type; for the younger Despoina, on a Late Classical; for the Titan Anytos, on a high Hellenistic type.[5] Even if the models are quite heavily overlaid by Damophon's own personal style, their diverse provenances and their determination by subject cannot be missed.

So, too, the composition of the neo-Attic relief kraters of the Pisa type (*ca.* 100 BC) originates in a Greek workshop.[6] Here the Dionysiac *thiasos* is put together from elements of the most varied origin: Dionysos and his entourage from late Hellenistic figure-types, which also occur in the composition of the so-called Ikarios relief (*ca.* 100 BC);[7] the dancing women, by contrast, from a Late Classical group of dancing nymphs, one figure of which is (to complete the story) replaced by one of the maenads from a well-known cycle of the late fifth century. For the ecstatic female dance, the waving forms of the late fifth and fourth centuries provided the best prototype; for the exuberance of the satyrs, Hellenistic realism; all then reworked for this late Hellenistic, neo-Attic composition.

This handling of artistic forms was quickly transmitted by Greek artists to Rome, which was then developing into a centre of Hellenistic art. The famous figure of an Apollo, which was made in the mid-second century BC by the Athenian sculptor Timarchides for the Temple of Apollo *in Circo* (plate 49),[8] looked back to the Late Classical Apollo Lykeios type; its posture was evidently regarded as an especially convincing portrayal of the divine calm and youthful beauty of Apollo's appearance. At the same period, however, portraits of the leading personalities in Rome were being executed in Hellenistic style: such as the so-called Thermae Ruler (second quarter second century BC) who, from his find-spot in Rome and his lack of a diadem, must probably represent one of the leading Romans of the mid-second century (plate 50).[9] This contrast can be generalised: since the adoption of the latest Greek stylistic forms in the early second century BC, cult-statues in temples of the gods in Rome had generally been modelled on the Classical Greek style, portraits by contrast on a continuation of the Hellenistic.[10] The choice of Hellenistic or classicising forms and models can therefore express neither the general taste of this epoch, nor that of this cultural group, nor the attitude of individual clients either: for, all in all, it was the same men who were founding the temples and being honoured with portrait-statues. The differences here follow from the subject represented: for the worship of the gods, *maiestas* and *pondus* were the definitive answer; for the leading politicians, dynamic energy in the tradition of Alexander and the Diadochi.

Especially pointed is the contemporary use of heterogeneous forms for two heads, both of which belong to state monuments in Rome itself, for the victories over the Cimbri and Teutones, and so were

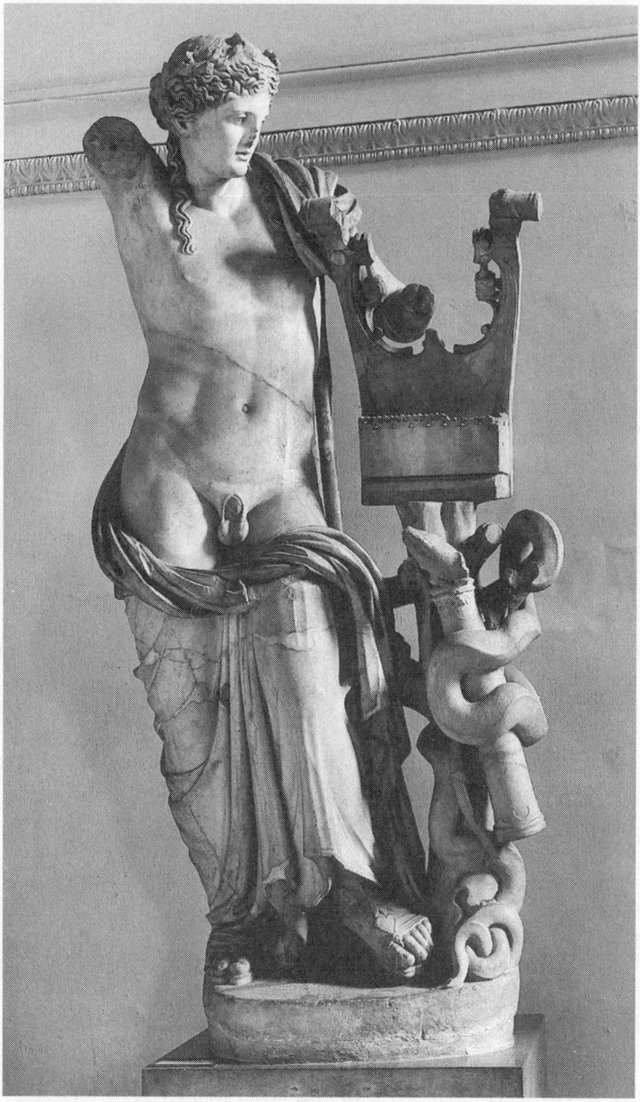

Plate 49: Statue of Apollo, copy of Antonine period from Cyrene of the Apollo *in Circo* of Timarchides

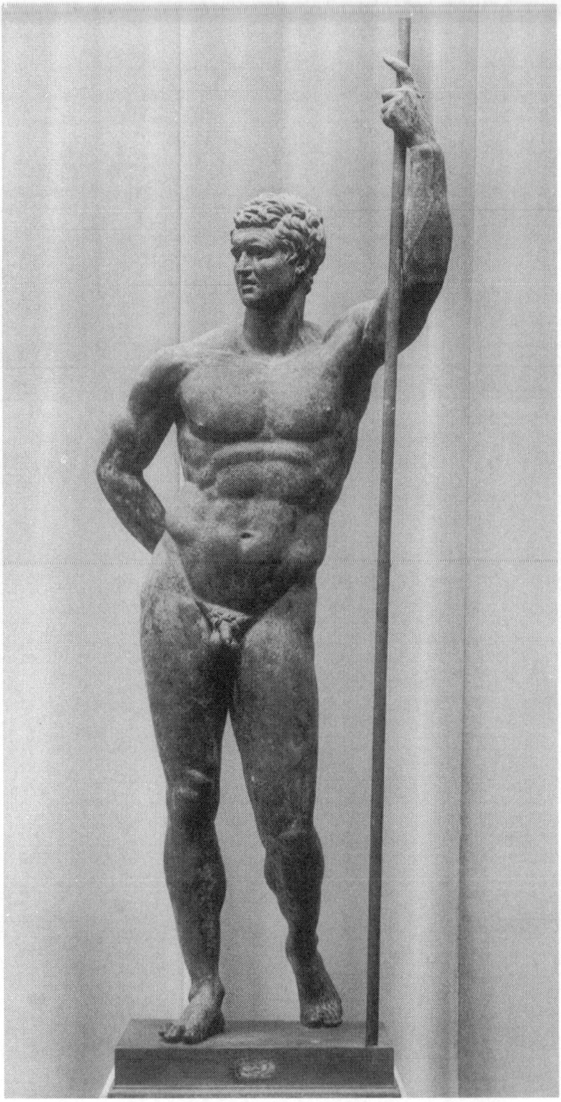

Plate 50: Portrait statue of a Roman, so-called 'Thermae Ruler', second quarter second century BC

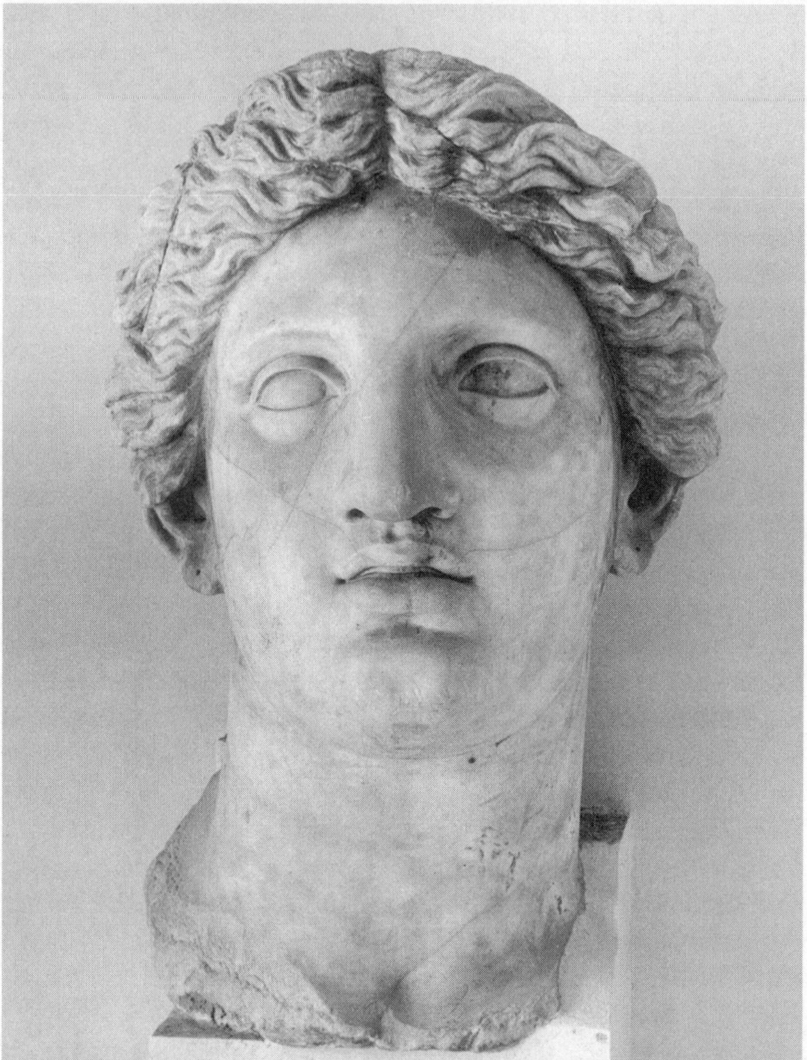

Plate 51: Head of cult-statue, Fortuna *huiusce diei*, *ca.* 100 BC

set up around 100 BC. In the Temple of Fortuna of this Day (*huiusce diei*), which Q. Lutatius Catulus built in the Porticus Minucia (Largo Argentina) in thanksgiving for the victory at Vercellae in 101 BC, the colossal cult-statue exhibited a calm language of imagery in the manner of the fourth century BC (plate 51).[11] On the other hand a head in Brussels, which from its knot of hair over the temple must represent a German and, to judge from its style, must belong to a metropolitan monument from the same victory, extends the tradition of Hellenistic barbarian figures (plate 52).[12] Here, already, a pathetic form of representation exemplifies the theme of war and the misery of defeat, directly beside the style of Classical grandeur in the figure of the goddess.

Yet the differences in formal tradition cannot be understood as the styles of different workshops either – as has already been demonstrated, for the Greek sphere, by the kraters of the Pisa type which combine heterogeneous elements in one and the same work. A similar treatment of style can be deduced from the written sources on the sculptor Pasiteles, the leading artist in Rome in the first half of the first century BC.[13] This man – born in southern Italy and made a Roman citizen after the Social War, whose very biography exemplifies to perfection the crystallisation of Greek culture in Rome – brought together and documented his extensive art-historical education in a five-volume work on *The Noble Works in the Whole World* (*opera nobilia in toto orbe*).[14] His Jupiter of ivory, on grounds of its material alone, probably stood in the tradition of the colossal cult-statues of Pheidias (*ca.* 430 BC).[15] His workshop's connection with the early Classical style of Greece is shown by the famous figure of a youth, made by his pupil Stephanos, perhaps a copy of an actual work by his master.[16] On the other hand, Pasiteles is said to have drawn the lions in their cages at the harbour of Rome,[17] which probably points to a study of nature of a Hellenistic kind; and finally he portrayed, in relief silverwork, a dramatic episode from the life of Roscius,[18] evidently in the tradition of Hellenistic narrative imagery. Here too, the selection of different modes of representation was totally dictated by the subject.

The range of formal resources was continually widened, during the second and first centuries BC, by the progressive annexation of the past

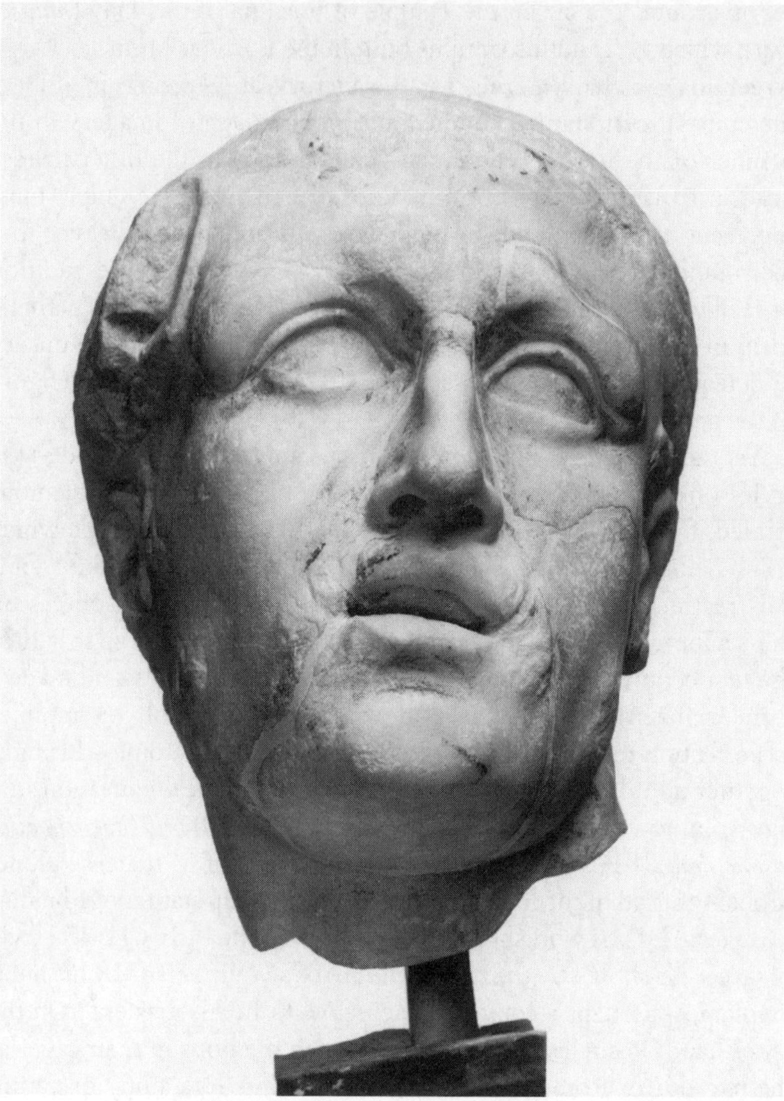

Plate 52: Head of a German, *ca.* 100 BC

history of art. In this process, the artists probably had no conscious vision of a semantic system in mind, either at the outset or later. Rather, the forms were probably selected, added to and reinforced one by one, flexibly and spontaneously, according to their power to convince.

But by Augustan times at the latest, the repertory of forms must have achieved a certain completeness.[19] Thereafter, individual cases of new imagery must have come into being, as well as new directions of choice and emphasis; but all in all, at least during the first two centuries of the Imperial period, the semantic system seems to have been more or less static in character. At the most, a much longer-term change arose from the increasingly routine standardisation of the language of imagery, which went together with the mass-production of sculpture for display. We see a fossilisation of the language of imagery, corresponding to the increasing standardisation of its themes.

NOTES

1. This phenomenon, to which Himmelmann drew my attention, deserves closer investigation.
2. Harrison (1965) 61ff., esp. 64; Willers (1975), 66f.
3. Above, pp. 87–8.
4. Below, pp. 125–6ff.
5. Dickins (1905–6); (1906–7); (1910–11); Becatti (1940) 7–116, esp. 40ff. On the Demeter: Becatti (1951) pls. 2.5, 6.17 (in so far as it is ancient); Schrader (1924) fig. 300. On the Despoina: Rizzo (1932) pls. 135ff.; Schmidt (1970) 29ff. pls. 31–33, figs. 3–11. On the Anytos, Schmidt (1961) pls. 44, 47, 49.
6. Merlin and Poinssot (1930) 41ff.; Fuchs (1959) 157f.; (1963) 45f. Most recently, Grassinger (1991).
7. Watzinger (1946–7).
8. Becatti (1935) and (1940), esp. 33f.; Coarelli (1968), esp. 331ff.; (1970–1), esp. 250ff.; La Rocca (1977); Simon (1984) 383, no. 61. Simon rightly points out that Vitr., *De arch.*, 10.2.13 cannot, as Coarelli thinks, be connected with the Temple of Apollo in Rome, and rejects the identification with the Apollo of Timarchides. I see the colossal hand-fragment (La Rocca (1977)), for which no other possible restoration exists, as a reinforcement of Becatti's argument. If the type at first found no successors in the west (Simon (1984) 383), then Simon's explanation (p. 384), that since Augustus' time a different idealisation of the god had come to prevail, could still stand if the original were in Rome. And especially if one can no longer believe that traders are shown on the relief of the Arch of Beneventum, then a local connection with

the god of the temple becomes possible once more. Becatti's interpretation is taken up and extended by Martin (1987) 64ff. Besides, the dating of the original need not be placed immediately after 179 BC: the new building, then decided on, was probably only executed towards the middle of the second century.

9. Buschor (1949) 31f.; Zanker (1973) 37, 40.
10. On temple cult-statues in general, Martin (1987) *passim*. On portraits of politicians, Zanker (1973) 34ff. and (1976). Giuliani (1986).
11. Marchetti-Longhi (1932–3); Helbig[4] II, no. 1673 (E. Simon); Coarelli (1968) 367, n.203 and (1981) 20 and 38ff., pl. 7; Martin (1987) 103ff.
12. Hölscher (1984a) 283–94.
13. On Pasiteles in general, Borda (1953), esp. 18ff.
14. Plin., *HN* 36.39.
15. Plin., *HN* 36.40.
16. Zanker (1974) 49ff. The design is usually attributed to Pasiteles' pupil Stephanos, who signed the figure in the Villa Albani. Since, however, this figure has a more simplified body than appears in other replicas, and in the head, too, hardly represents the finest tradition (Zanker (1973)), it might easily belong to a lesser branch in the stemma of copies. For this reason, I consider the attribution of the original to Pasiteles very probable.
17. Plin., *HN* 36.40.
18. Cic., *Div.* 1.36.79.
19. On this compare Zanker (1979); the same author in *Classicisme*, 283–306; Hölscher (1980a); Cain (1985) 148; Maderna (1987); Grassinger (1991).

CHAPTER 10

Language of imagery and style

Although the language of imagery had soon reached the condition of a certain fixity, yet time did not stand still: for tastes changed. But what place was there, within the system of forms of Roman art, for period-specific changes? And how were such changes related to the relatively static language of imagery?

This is where the categories of type and style come into their own.[1] The language of imagery, which had been developed out of heterogeneous elements and then retained a more or less static validity, was essentially typological in its nature. Collective tastes, on the other hand, which unite those belonging to the same epoch, the same cultural region or the same social group, independently of individual subjects, and which then change correspondingly as one moves from any one of these to the next, are crystallised in the phenomenon of style. As with language, where the freedom for stylistic expression can avail itself of a firm basis of vocabulary, forms and rules, so both features are present with imagery too: representational types offer the subject-based, and therefore durably established, formulae, while stylistic execution is the expression of a general taste and attitude. According to the subject, one could take up models from a choice of various epochs of Greek art, and thereby still present the heterogeneous elements as a unified style.

One might ask how it was possible for so important a part of design as the formation of types to be largely excluded from the sphere of stylistic expression, and relegated to that of semantics. This question of course arises out of a modern, absolute conception of style as the logical expression of the artist as agent. For the Romans, the phenomenon of 'style' did not have this radical force for every aspect of a work.

One can clarify this problem for oneself, on a theoretical level, from Cicero's position.[2] Anyone who, like Cicero, rejected emotional forms of rhetoric and approved of the measured classical style of speaking, because it was more appropriate for the dignity of a Roman office-bearer, could draw two different conclusions from this: either this was a decision in favour of a general attitude, in the widest sense; in which case, one must cut out all Hellenistic traditions aimed at effects of pathos, and replace them with classicising forms. Or it applied to a specific sphere: in which case classicising forms of style were only to be demanded where the *auctoritas* and *gravitas* of Roman dignitaries were to find expression. Accordingly, Cicero's contemporary C. Licinius Calvus composed his public speeches in a severely Atticising manner, after the style of the Athenian orators of the fourth century BC, while his poems were by contrast in the Alexandrian style of the neoterics.[3]

Both conclusions had a certain justification, and both found their counterparts in the practice of sculptors. Compared to the dignity of state ceremonies, warfare had to be depicted with pathos and arduousness – yet the general ideal of measured dignity was not to be entirely breached. But they could be combined with each other, the different modes of representation and the general ideal, because the two basic assumptions were not equally ranked: on one side, a specific pattern of behaviour in one restricted area of life, on the other a comprehensive, and therefore superior, ideal. Thus the two kinds of message belong to different levels in the work of art. The subject-based choice of models belongs to the sphere of patterns of representation and figural forms; the general ideal to the level of stylistic execution. It was style that made it possible, for each period, region or group, to compose from the heterogeneous semantic elements an integrated set of attitudes, and thereby to differentiate itself from other periods, regions and groups. The generally static semantic system thus acquired an aspect of collective change.

It is not possible here systematically to separate out those aspects of artistic form which were susceptible of stylistic change. The scope that remained for this was relatively small, since the modes and types of representation were to a great extent thematically prescribed. On the Aeneas relief of the Ara Pacis, the relief style of the Augustan workshop, which integrates the heterogeneous typological traditions, achieves its effect in two main ways: in the firm attachment of figures and objects to the flat surface, so that all the motifs are articulated in clear outlines; and in the lively animation of the marble-working, which at the same time is executed with severe clarity. In the Augustan period, this treatment of relief and modelling of surface, taken together, were doubtless meant to evoke, regardless of the origins of the typological elements, a 'classical' impression, which conformed to the ideology and taste of the Augustan court. In Flavian times, on the other hand, the intentional recourse to more realistic form and less stylised attitudes had the effect of a certain *rapprochement* to Hellenistic relief style. Not only the semantic figural types, but the stylistic attitude as well, can take a lead from Greek models.

Some of the questions which arise from this can only be intimated here. Undoubtedly, the taste and ideology of different epochs and regions can not only put their stamp on the collective style but, in addition, penetrate to other levels of the work of art as well, that is in the choice of subjects and types. From the fact that figural types were not determined, with complete rigidity, by the subjects of the imagery,[4] there arose the possibility of selecting typological models, too, in such a way as allowed the clearest possible realisation of the stylistic tendencies of the time. It is no coincidence that, apart from the continuing Hellenistic tradition of massed battle-scenes, there is preserved from early Augustan times, on the frieze of the Temple of Apollo *in Circo*, one of the few battle-representations which looks back to the Classical manner of composition in separate groups of combatants.[5] That copies of the works of Polykleitos are known, above all, from the Julio-Claudian and Hadrianic periods, but are rare in Flavian times, points in the same direction.[6] Future research will have to investigate in detail how far the authority of such points of view extended.

To judge from the overall results, however, this aspect of the choice of typological models according to changing tastes, so heavily emphasised in earlier research, has undoubtedly only a relative importance. For in so far as it is applicable at all, the period-specific element of choice applies not only to the forms, but to the subjects as well: in contrast with the admiration for Polykleitan youths in Julio-Claudian and Hadrianic times, not only the Polykleitan model of form, but the whole genre of youthful males, fell into the background in the second half of the first century AD. The semantic aspect is thus in every case the predominant one. For the bulk of production, however, it is certainly the case that the different subjects and the heterogeneous types of representation in principle retained their validity across the boundaries of period and region.[7]

Significant in this context is the portrait, as an extreme case for the relationship between type and style.[8] No other medium displays a dynamic of development that is so strongly period-specific as this; all attempts to establish a framework of temporal styles for Roman art take the portrait as their starting-point. Admittedly, even with portraits, thematic and typological aspects played a considerable part, with forms of diverse origins being used to convey messages with different types of content, crossing the boundaries of stylistic epochs; this is especially clear in Augustan times, with the use of a Classical language of imagery for the portraits of the court, and its simultaneous diffusion side by side with the continued use of Republican forms in the representation of freedmen.[9] All in all, however, the truly dominant factor here is that of temporal style, and of an ideal, definitive 'face for the age'.[10] The question arises whether this separate status for the portrait can be plausibly located within the system as a whole.

If the factor of temporal style comes out so much more strongly in the portrait than in other artistic media, such as idealising sculpture, then this brings out the fact that this subject was more responsive than other fields of artistic production to the experiences of changing ages. Evidently, within a world of images, which was becoming more and more an inventory of symbols for abstract conceptions, the persona of the human agent was felt to be the one concrete reality. A characteristic example is the relief, from the series on the Arch of Constantine, of the entry of Marcus Aurelius into Rome (AD 176).[11] The ruler is flanked by Mars and Roma, and in addition by personifications, probably Felicitas ('Good Fortune') and Aeternitas ('Eternity'), representatives, that is, of a traditional ideology. This system of values was abstract, collective and relatively static, and so found an adequate formulation in stereotyped, traditional, idealised figures. Only the portrait of the ruler (which has been restored in the baroque style) must have stood out from its setting through its individualised physiognomy: in his person, the system of values turned into reality.

Through this specific connection with reality, the portrait became distinctively a field for the operation of a many-sided, and also a changing, experience of life. This is evidently the reason why this medium possessed, to a much higher degree than most other categories of Roman art, a dynamic of stylistic development: amid the stasis of the generally abstract dominant images, the individual became the most sensitive seismograph of historical change. Whereas, in the other subjects of imagery, standardised messages were formulated in an almost canonical repertory of patterns and types, and represented the attitude of their period only in respect of their 'style', so the portrait represented relatively pure 'attitude', and was thus to a greater degree dictated by 'style'. This means that even the specific realism of the portrait as such, with its strong susceptibility to change, has its precise place in the clearly defined semantic system of the Roman language of imagery.

Past research, with its preconceived interest in historical change, has pushed the portrait, as an indicator of stylistic development, very much to the fore in general interest. With other genres such as historical relief or idealising sculpture, under this same premiss, it has strongly isolated and emphasised the dynamic and stylistic phenomena at the expense of the typological and static aspects. This is obviously a limited way of looking at things: such an approach covers one specific genre above all, and only a narrow aspect of the other genres. If this approach conceals the typological stasis, then that is no mere isolated phenomenon of form; access to an important achievement of Roman art as a language of imagery, that is as a resource for visual communication, is thereby obstructed; and the distinctive characteristic of Roman Imperial culture, its far-reaching constancy, never even comes into view.

If Roman idealising sculpture has hitherto proved difficult of access for stylistic dating, we should see in this not merely a regrettable fact that needs to be surmounted – which it certainly is – but also a significant phenomenon: in Roman art, change is less general, less fundamental and less rapid than it is in Greek art from the Archaic to the Hellenistic period. A sophisticated understanding of Roman art will need to set off against each other, as far as is possible, the static and the dynamic elements, as functions of a corresponding purpose in each case, in a wider historical context. One such fundamental element, on the static side, is the semantic system of the language of imagery.[12]

NOTES

1. Above, pp. 11–14f.
2. Above, p. 47.
3. Schanz and Hosius (1927) 289f., 392ff.; Bowersock in *Classicisme*, 63, already noted by Zanker (ibid., 77) as a parallel for sculptural practice.
4. Above, pp. 97–8f.
5. Chapter 5, n.11.
6. Lauter (1969) 129; Zanker (1974) 41.
7. So previously Zanker in *Classicisme*, 301.
8. On what follows, see Hölscher (1982).
9. Zanker (1975).
10. On the phenomenon of the 'face for the age' (*Zeitgesicht*), Zanker (1982).
11. Scott Ryberg (1967) pl. 23; Hölscher (1980a) 321.
12. Here again, these conclusions on form represent a companion-piece to the structure of content of Roman state reliefs: Hölscher (1980a) 315ff.

CHAPTER II

Formal system and style in the theory of rhetoric and of imagery

The system here described seems to have little correspondence with the picture given by the explicit testimony of the sources for Roman Classicism. Classicising art theory is aimed not so much at the thematically oriented selection of various styles, as at a general return to the high point of Classical art, which had been set up as a norm in the absolute sense. Certainly the two positions – Greek tradition on the one hand as a basic, 'classical' attitude to life, on the other as an available language of imagery of heterogeneous provenance – are not to be treated as mutually exclusive alternatives: both are too well attested for that. But an understanding of the phenomena is to be measured according to its degree of success in reconciling the two positions.

Quintilian shows us one route to understanding, when he discusses the classification of rhetorical styles in association with those of imagery. His position here is based on classicising art theory of later Hellenistic times.[1]

The sphere of imagery involves the different possibilities of form which had been developed in the past – that is, kinds of style (*genera*) which are differentiated according to epochs, regions and artistic personalities. These various forms are judged by a typical mixture of absolute and relative standards.

On the one hand, there is an established progression from the imperfect beginnings to the absolute high points: perfection is represented in Greek sculpture by Polykleitos and Pheidias; from the not quite so highly rated standpoint of *veritas*, by Praxiteles and Lysippos; in painting, Zeuxis, Parrhasios and later Apelles occupy the highest position. Form is the only standard; its evaluation is undertaken from a basically classicising standpoint.

On the other hand, each style was also credited with its own specific achievement, which is denoted by abstract expressions.[2] Protogenes excels in *cura*, Antiphilos in *facilitas*, Apelles in *ingenium* and *gratia*. It is informative here that, with sculptors, such diverse potential is in part tied to specific subject-matter: Polykleitos was the master of *diligentia* and *decor*, so he is recognised as being the most important sculptor for human, especially youthful figures. On the other hand, he was excelled by Pheidias and Alkamenes in their capacity to endow their figures with *pondus* and to portray dignified maturity; thus they gave better expression to the *auctoritas* and *maiestas* of the gods. Here again, it is true that the Classical period of the fifth and fourth centuries is obligatory in terms of absolute framework; but the merits of the individual artists are in part placed side by side, as specific attainments without a ranking order, and in part relativised by being linked to specific subject-matter.

The classicising theory of art on which this is based combined both programmes at once, in that it arranged the various artistic themes on a scale which was consistent with the rise of art, in terms of the history of style, to its high point of Classicism: Kalamis and Myron for animals, Polykleitos for youthful figures, Pheidias and Alkamenes for gods. The hierarchy and history of style was at the same time a hierarchy and history of subject. The contrived artificiality of the system is obvious. It stems from the failure to realise that a fundamental conflict had arisen here, between a diachronic scheme of development and a range of expressive values and subjects that was in principle ahistorical.[3]

So for the reception of these models in the practice of Roman figural art, this diachronic aspect of the conception was itself irrelevant. The various subjects, and with them the 'best' forms to represent them, were here required contemporaneously and side by side: in reality, the range of themes in question, from animal to deity, has a systematic and synchronic, not a historical and diachronic character. If Roman art wanted to bring the whole diversity of current subjects into the picture, and at the same time insisted on the exemplary quality of models of various periods for specific subjects, then the historicity of the stylistic forms had to fade into the background.[4]

The transformation of the diachronic succession of exemplary artists, with their subjects, into a synchronic system of elements of form and content can be detected in Quintilian, not in his sections on imagery, but in his discussion of rhetorical style. Here Quintilian's starting-point is the tripartite division of the Attic, Asianic and, lying between the two, Rhodian movements, that is, the polarity between Attic Classicism and the Hellenistic style of Asia Minor.[5] In their origins, these are styles of different epochs, but for Quintilian they are available side by side, as diametrically opposed options for contemporary rhetorical style: out of a diachronic succession, a synchronic field of possibilities has come into being, between which the orator has to make a fundamental choice. Here Quintilian unambiguously places himself on the side of the Atticists. Later, however, he introduces a further classification, again into three categories: the *genus subtile*, the *genus robustum*, with a *genus floridum* between the two.[6] These three types of style are, however, to be used alongside one another, according to theme, occasion and the desired effect.[7] In this context, it is thus of special interest that the two sets of categories have certain connections with each other: the *genus subtile* possesses qualities which, above all, were important for the Atticising movement; the *genus robustum*, by contrast, unexpectedly contains, to some extent on the positive side, certain qualities which had been cited for the Asianic movement.[8] Not that Quintilian, or anyone else, would have wished to build a bridge between the Asianic movement and the *genus robustum*: but the fact of this partial affinity betrays the condition on which many features of the Asianic tradition could become acceptable, though admittedly only under other, less disadvantageous names. Here too, elements of the styles of various periods could thus become simultaneously available components of an extensive language of forms;[9] and here too these components are in essence semantically determined.

For Quintilian, admittedly, this palette of possibilities is subordinated to his fundamental prior judgment in favour of Atticism. This is his real 'style'; in this spirit, the 'Asianic' elements too are in his view to be played down and integrated into the unified, overall attitude.[10] Here, then, rhetoric is divided between two levels: on one, various traditions are employed according to objective need; on the other, personal attitude is recognisable through an unambiguous choice.

Quintilian, in keeping with his didactic aim, does not work out in detail the transference of these ideas to the sphere of imagery. But in fact the phenomena, as such, find their clear counterparts in the structure of the work of art. Clearly, Quintilian's two levels, that of the various *genera* on the one hand, and that of the general attitude to style on the other, correspond very precisely with the distinction, in imagery, between available semantic types and general style. The levels can perhaps be even more securely distinguished in the works of art than in a linguistic text.

Classicising art theory, on which Quintilian bases himself, can already be recognised in Cicero and, in fragmentary form, in Pliny too: similar assumptions can be found first in the *Auctor ad Herennium*, then later in Dionysios of Halikarnassos and Lucian.[11] In so far as art was reflected on at all, this was the dominant outlook in the late Republic and in Imperial times. This outlook led everywhere to a conjunction of the scheme of diachronic development with a system of formal and ethical concepts of effect, which in turn were assigned to specific subject-areas. In no case did the authors show any realisation that the historical sequence had thereby, in the reception of the present day, become relativised – yet the tendency is unmistakably in this direction. In the theoretical field too, the semanticisation of style took place.

The anonymous author of the *Rhetorica ad Herennium* moves especially close to the working procedure of the sculptor.[12] As an absurd analogy for an eclectic orator, he points out how Chares, when Lysippos showed him a head by Myron, arms by Praxiteles and a torso by Polykleitos as models, still did not learn the sculptor's art from him. Here we evidently strike a common late Hellenistic notion, in so far as the names of the artists stand for the styles of their respective epochs. Here too, however, the models are not picked out at random, but are chosen according to their specific excellence in respect of the relevant part of the body – that is, thematically: Polykleitos' strength was seen as lying in the construction of his bodies, that of Late Classicism in the natural mobility of the limbs, that of the Severe Style no doubt in the *ethos* of the facial expressions and in the precision and richness of the hair. The extant works of late Hellenistic eclecticism show that this semantic filter was admittedly not absolutely canonical, but in many ways it led the choice of models in this direction.[13]

NOTES

1. Quint., *Inst.* 12.10.1ff., on which see Robert (1886) 47ff.; Schweitzer (1932) 32ff.; Austin (1944) and (1948) 135ff. On the relationship between rhetoric and aesthetics in general, see also Bialostocky (1982) 11ff.
2. Schweitzer (1932) 36ff.
3. It is striking that this internal contradiction, between diachronic historical reconstruction and synchronic experience of life, has apparently not been noted in previous research: a result of the exclusive concentration on the concept of developmental history.
4. See above, p. 96.
5. Quint., *Inst.* 12.10.16ff.
6. Quint., *Inst.* 12.10.58ff. For a collection of sources on the three *genera*, their specific achievements, subjects, peculiarities and risks: Lausberg (1960) 519ff.
7. Quint., *Inst.* 12.10.69ff. Very vividly at 78: 'brilliant, lofty and opulent, he (the orator) has command over the (military) forces of eloquence that flow around him'.
8. I was surprised not to find, in the current handbooks and studies of Quintilian, recognition of the proximity between the *genus robustum* and the Asianic movement. Yet it seems to me quite obvious: compare on the one hand Quint., *Inst.* 12.10 §§12, 16–19, 73 (on Asianic rhetoric); on the other, §§22–4 (on the richer, typically later Attic orators of the fourth century, whom Quintilian uses to justify Cicero's rhetorical richness), §§36, 45–52 (on the forms of style which Quintilian considers desirable for Roman rhetoric), §§59–65, 69–72 (on the potential of the *genus robustum*). Even the descriptions and metaphors can be alike: 'swirling torrents' (*torrentes turbidi*; §19, Asianic rhetoric) – 'a river, abundant and in torrent, which rolls away rocks and disdains a bridge and creates its own banks for itself' (*amnis qui saxa devolvat et pontem indignetur et ripas sibi faciat multus et torrens*; §61, *genus robustum*); 'overflowing' (*abundantes*; §18, the Asianics) – 'amplification', 'exaggeration' (*amplificatio, superlatio*; §62, *genus robustum*). The citations can be multiplied if one goes beyond Quintilian. In a similar way, the boundaries between the Asianic movement and the *genus robustum* were contested. Cicero was branded as an Asianic by purist Atticists, on grounds of stylistic methods which belonged to the *genus robustum*: Quint., *Inst.* 12.10.12ff. Apart from this, too, there was consciousness of the danger that *hupsos* and *megaloprepeia*, both qualities belonging to the *genus robustum*, could degenerate into bombast:

Martin (1974) 334, 336. Compare too Quint., *Inst.* 12.10.80. None of this is changed by the fact that each orator subjectively believed that he could recognise the boundaries.

9. It will become clear from what follows that, in Quintilian and in conceptions similar to his, the basically developmental historical phenomenon of the change from Classical simplicity to ever-increasing richness is overlaid by the system of the synchronic *genera*. The orthodox Atticists kept to the factual, reticent style of Lysias and, from this standpoint, accused Cicero of being an Asianic; his richer style of oratory was justified by Quintilian, by reference to the style of Demosthenes (see n.8). In the system of the *genera*, these stylistic options then correspond to the *genus subtile* and the *genus robustum*. Demosthenes, as the last Classical Athenian, was an unassailable name, through whom forms could be justified down to the very brink of the Hellenistic 'decline'. A similar rôle, in figural art, is played by Lysippos and his school (above, p. 94).
10. Quint., *Inst.* 12.10.79f., in repetition of 12.10.16ff. Likewise with the theory and practice of historiography, above, p. 45.
11. See in general Schweitzer (1932) 32ff.; Cic., *Brut.* 18, 70; compare *De orat.* 3.26; Schweitzer (1932); Becatti (1951) 96ff. Dionysios of Halikarnassos: *Isoc.* 3. Pliny: Schweitzer (1932). Lucian, *Imagines* 6; Preisshofen and Zanker (1970–1), esp. 108ff. In general, Andò (1975), esp. 80ff. *Auctor ad Herennium*: see following note.
12. *Rhet. Her.*, 4.6.9; Preisshofen and Zanker (1970–1) 100ff.
13. So Preisshofen and Zanker (1970–1) 112ff.

CHAPTER 12

Conclusion: language of imagery and culture of empire

The distinctive achievement of the system of forms in Roman art was that it was capable of fulfilling both the demands of an educated élite and the needs of the population of the Empire at large. The language of imagery could equally serve as an expression of cultured historical background and élitist way of life, and as a universally understood system of visual communication.

There is a clear connection between these two aspects. The celebrated masterpieces of Greek art came to be the recognised norms for specific subjects and messages of content. Accordingly they acquired, in Roman art as well, a far-reaching validity for their relevant subject-areas. But the greater the validity that the 'norm' achieved, the more 'normal' it became.[1] The forms of the models developed, through redundancy in their use, into commonplace formulae which designated things, rather than establishing norms. They might at first have complied with high intellectual standards; but because of their status as models, and provided that they were convincing, they acquired a general distribution: they became 'self-explanatory'. The concentration on 'classical' models thus turned into a common, rehearsed and often trivial practice. There is a seamless transition from the cultured values of the ruling class to the general language of imagery of the Empire's population. Here lies the reason for the fact that, alongside highly sensitive copies and new creations in traditional styles, an enormous number of Roman works in the Greek tradition are of very ordinary quality, whose aim was certainly not to be seen as reflecting the greatness of Greece, but rather as representing themes of imagery which were important to the population as a whole. In such conditions, what mattered was not necessarily the origins of the forms, in terms of the history of style, and doubtless even their connection with values frequently came to be lost. The received forms were allowed to become value-free elements in a language of imagery, which one simply used. In the course of contemporary practice, art-historical understanding and theoretical reflection came to be more and more irrelevant.

Yet this was not simply an irreversible development in one single direction. Something which had become a common, standard formula could at any time be consciously refashioned, with sensitivity, to exemplify a higher norm and be understood as such. Thus arose the long-lasting ambivalence of Roman 'classicising', as between an élitist attitude and an omnipresent Imperial culture.

This universally dispersed and intelligible language of imagery was of great importance in terms of cultural history. It had rapidly fused into a complex but relatively accessible system of visual communication. This system then retained a more or less constant validity, despite some changes of detail, for about two centuries after the beginning of the Imperial period. It was a means of communication of universally recognised validity and transparency.

But if this language of imagery was to function as a general means of visual communication, then its routine quality and general absence of 'creativity', which for the present-day understanding of 'art' might be seen as a cause for regret, were not a deficiency but a strength. The utility of a system of communication rests precisely in the fact that its formulae and syntax are familiar from constant repetition, offer as few surprises as possible, and thus become understandable. The – in many respects – static character of Roman art, the general absence of fundamental innovation, contributes decisively to the intelligibility of this language of imagery. But this also serves to bring out the historical function of that language: for it is obvious that such an easily understood and usable system of communication, particularly in so large and heterogeneous a form of state as the Roman *imperium*, must have responded to a pressing need.

If we nevertheless wish to take critical stock of this art, then that too is entirely legitimate.[2] It must, however, on the one hand start from a conscious position in the present; and secondly, it must not treat art in isolation, but must also involve its function in the Imperial culture, and the historical situation of that culture, as a whole. The visual language corresponds, in its ever-increasing standardisation, to the growing standardisation and ideal stereotyping of the visual message. The very fact that this is a largely unconscious process makes it a good gauge of the gradual fossilisation of Roman Imperial culture as a whole.

NOTES

1. For the fundamental functions, contexts of display and effects of Roman sculpture, see Zanker in *Classicisme*, 283–306, esp. 286f., 294f.
2. P. Zanker in *Classicisme*, 304ff.; Hölscher (1984c) 36f.

References

ABBREVIATIONS

AA = *Archäologischer Anzeiger*
AbhBerlin = *Abhandlungen der Preussischen Akademie der Wissenschaften zu Berlin, philosophisch-historische Klasse*
AbhGöttingen = *Abhandlungen der Akademie der Wissenschaften in Göttingen, philosophisch-historische Klasse*
AbhMainz = *Abhandlungen der Akademie der Wissenschaften und Literatur Mainz, philosophisch-historische Klasse*
AJA = *American Journal of Archaeology*
AM = *Mitteilungen des Deutschen Archäologischen Instituts, Athenische Abteilung*
AnalRom = *Analecta Romana Instituti Danici*
AntK = *Antike Kunst*
AntPl = *Antike Plastik*
AvP = *Altertümer von Pergamon*
BCom = *Bullettino della Commissione archeologica comunale di Roma*
BJb = *Bonner Jahrbücher*
BollMusRom = *Bollettino dei Musei comunali di Roma*
Brunn/Bruckmann = P. Arndt, *Brunn-Bruckmanns Denkmäler der Griechischer und Römischer Sculptur*, added volumes, 1902–47.
BSA = *The Annual of the British School at Athens*
BWPr = *Berliner Winckelmanns-Programm*
CQ = *The Classical Quarterly*
DArch = *Dialoghi di Archeologia*
HallWPr = *Hallisches Winckelmanns-Programm*
HAW = *Handbuch der Altertumswissenschaft*
HdArch = *Handbuch der Archäologie*
Helbig[4] = W. Helbig, *Führer durch die öffentlichen Sammlungen Klassischer Altertümer in Rom*, 4th edn, 1963–72
Historia = *Historia. Zeitschrift für Alte Geschichte*

JdI = *Jahrbuch des Deutschen Archäologischen Instituts*
JdI Erg.-H. = *Jahrbuch des Deutschen Archäologischen Instituts*, Ergänzungs-Heft
JRA = *Journal of Roman Archaeology*
JRS = *Journal of Roman Studies*
Klio = *Klio. Beiträge zur Alten Geschichte*
LIMC = *Lexicon Iconographicum Mythologiae Classicae*
MEFRA = *Mélanges de l'Ecole Française de Rome. Antiquité*
MemAmAc = *Memoirs of the American Academy in Rome*
MemPontAc = *Memorie della Pontificia Accademia Romana di archeologia*
NSc = *Notizie degli Scavi*
ÖJh = *Jahreshefte des Österreichischen Archäologischen Instituts in Wien*
OpRom = *Opuscula Romana*
Poetica = *Poetica. Zeitschrift für Sprach- und Literaturwissenschaft*
RE = *Paulys Realencyclopädie der klassischen Altertumswissenschaft*
REL = *Revue des études latines*
RIA = *Rivista dell'Istituto Nazionale d'archeologia e storia dell'arte*
RM = *Mitteilungen des Deutschen Archäologischen Instituts, Römische Abteilung*
SbMünchen = *Sitzungsberichte der Bayerischen Akademie der Wissenschaften München*
SymbOslo = *Symbolae Osloenses*
TAPA = *Transactions of the American Philological Association*

Ackerman, J. S. and Carpenter, R. (1963) *Art and Archaeology*
Alpers, S. (1979) 'Style is What You Make it: The Visual Arts Once Again' in: Lang (1979): 137–62
Andò, V. (1975) *Luciano critico d'arte*
Andreae, B. (1956) *Motivgeschichtliche Untersuchungen zu den römischen Schlachtsarkophagen*
(1977) *Das Alexandermosaik aus Pompeji*
Austin, R. G. (1944) '*Quintiliani institutionis oratoriae liber XII*'. *CQ* 38: 17–26
(1948) *Quintilian Book XII*
Avenarius, G. (1956) *Lukians Schrift zur Geschichtsschreibung*
Bal, M. and Bryson, N. (1991) 'Semiotics and Art History'. *Art Bulletin* 73: 174–208
Bartocchini, R. (1929) *Le terme di Lepcis* (*Africa Italiana*, vol. IV)
Becatti, G. (1935) 'Timarchides e l'Apollo qui tenet citharam'. *BComm* 63: 111–31
(1940) 'Attika – saggio sulla scultura attica dell'ellenismo'. *RIA* 7: 7–116
(1951) *Arte e gusto negli scrittori latini*
(1951) *Problemi fidiaci*

Bergmann, B. and Kondoleon, C. (eds.) (1999) *The Art of Ancient Spectacle* (*Studies in the History of Art* 56)
Belting, H. (1987) *The End of the History of Art?*
Berenson, B. (1902) 'The Rudiments of Connoisseurship' in: *The Study and Criticism of Italian Art*: 111–48
(1927) *Three Essays on Method*
Berve, H. (ed.) (1942) *Das neue Bild der Antike*, vol. II
Beschi, L. (1962) *I bronzetti romani di Montorio Veronese*
Bhabha, H. (1996) 'Postmodernism/Postcolonialism' in: Nelson and Shiff (1996): 307–22
Bialostocky, S. (1982) *Stil und Ikonographie* (2nd edition)
Bianchi Bandinelli (1936) 'Il problema dell'arte romano' in: *Enciclopedia Italiana* 29: 729–30
(1937) 'La "struttura": Un tentative di approfondimento critico'. *La Critica d'Arte* 2: 189–92
(1950) *Storicità dell'arte classica*
(1960) 'Römische Kunst, zwei Generationen nach Wickhoff'. *Klio* 38: 267–83 (= *Archeologia e cultura* (1979) 224–46)
(1967) 'Arte plebea'. *DArch* 1: 7–19
(1970) *Rome: The Centre of Power*
(1971) *Rome: The Late Empire*
(1976) *Introduzione all'archeologia classica*
(1978a) *Dall'ellenismo al'medioevo*
(1978b) *Klassische Archäologie*
(1979) 'Roma antica: arte' in: *Enciclopedia Garzanti* vol. IX: 933–40
(1961/1979) *Archeologia e cultura* (2nd edn 1979)
Bieber, M. (1967) 'A Monument for Guido Kaschnitz von Weinberg'. *AJA* 71: 361–86
Blanckenhagen, P. H. von (1942) 'Elemente der römischen Kunst am Beispiel des Flavischen Stils' in: Berve (1942) 310–41
Bonanno, A. (1976) *Portraits and Other Heads on Roman Historical Relief up to the Age of Septimius Severus*
Borbein, A. H. (1975) 'Die Ara Pacis. Geschichtliche Wirklichkeit und Programm'. *JdI* 90: 242–66
Borda, M. (1953) *La scuola di Pasiteles*
Bothmer, D. von (1957) *Amazons in Greek Art*
Bowman, A. K., Garnsey, P. and Rathbone, D. W. (eds.) (1996) *The Cambridge Ancient History*, vol. XI (2nd edn)
Brandenburg, H. (1979) 'Stilprobleme der frühchristlichen Sarkophagkunst Roms im 4. Jahrhundert. Volkskunst, Klassizismus, spätantiker Stil'. *RM* 86: 439–71

(1981) 'Ars humilis. Zur Frage eines christlichen Stils in der Kunst des 4. Jahrhunderts nach Christus'. *Jahrbuch für Antike und Christentum* 24: 71–84

Brendel, O. J. (1930) 'Immolatio boum'. *RM* 45: 196–226

(1936) 'Gli studi sul rilievo storico romano in Germania'. *Studi Romani nel Mondo* 3: 122–44

(1953) 'Prolegomena to a Book on Roman Art'. *MemAmAc* 21: 7–73

(1979) *Prolegomena to the Study of Roman Art*

(1982) *Introduzione all'arte romana* (ed. S. Settis)

Brilliant, R. (2000) *My Laocoon: Alternative Claims in the Interpretation of Artworks*

Brommer, F. (1977) *Der Parthenonfries*

Brooker, P. (1992) *Modernism/Postmodernism*

Bryson, N., Holly, M. A. and Moxey, K. (eds.) (1991) *Visual Theory*

Buitron Oliver, D. (ed.) (1997) *The Interpretation of Architectural Sculpture in Greece and Rome* (*Studies in the History of Art* 49)

Bulard, M. (1926) 'Description des revêtements peints à sujets religieux' in: *Exploration archéologique de Délos*, vol. IX

Burck, E. (1964) *Die Erzählungskunst des Titus Livius*

Buschor, E. (1949) *Das hellenistische Bildnis*

Cagiano de Azavedo, M. (1951) *Le antichità di Villa Medici*

Cain, H. U. (1985) *Römische Marmorkandelaber*

Calo, M. A. (1993) *Bernard Berenson and the Twentieth Century*

Casson, S. (1921) *Catalogue of the Acropolis Museum*, vol. II

Cheetham, M. A., Holly, M. A. and Moxey, K. (eds.) (1988) *The Subjects of Art History*

Cichorius C. (1896–1900) *Die Reliefs der Traianssäule*

Clairmont, Chr. W. (1966) *Die Bildnisse des Antinous*

Classicisme = Fondation Hardt, *Entretiens sur l'antiquité classique* 25: *Le Classicisme à Rome aux 1ers siècles avant et après J.-C.* (1979)

Coarelli, F. (1968) 'L'"ara di Domizio Enobarbo" e la cultura artistica in Roma nel II secolo a.C.'. *DArch* 2: 302–68

(1970–1) 'Classe dirigente romana e arti figurative'. *DArch* 4–5: 241–65

(1978) 'Il "grande donario di Attalo I"' in: *I Galli e l'Italia* (Exhibition, Rome) 231–55

(1982) 'L'"agora des Italiens" a Delo: il mercato degli schiavi?'. *Opuscula Instituti Romani Finlandiae* 2: 119–45

Conkey, M. W. and Hastorf, C. A. (eds.) (1990) *The Uses of Style in Archaeology*

Conlin, D. (1997) *The Artists of the Ara Pacis*

Connor, W. (1984) *Thucydides*

Conze, A. and Puchstein, O. (1891) *Königliche Museen zu Berlin. Beschreibung der antiken Skulpturen*

Crimp, D. (1993) *On the Museum's Ruins*

Cutler, A. (1996) 'Byzantine Art and the North: Meditations on the Notion of Influence' in: *Byzantium, Identity, Image, Influence. XIX International Congress of Byzantine Studies, Major Papers*

D'Ambra, E. (ed.) (1993) *Roman Art in Context*

Davis, W. (1990) 'Style and History in Art History' in: Conkey and Hastorf (1990): 18–31

Del Vita, A. (1934) 'Ara marmorea trovata presso Porta Crucifera'. *NSc*: 429–33

Denti, M. (1985) 'Arte romana e cultura moderna: Le ragioni di una traduzione'. *Quaderni di Storia* 21: 141–54

Dickins, G. (1905–6) 'Damophon of Messene'. *BSA* 12: 109–36

(1906–7) 'Damophon of Messene II'. *BSA* 13: 357–404

(1910–11) 'Damophon of Messene III'. *BSA* 17: 80–7

Diehl, E. (1964) *Die Hydria. Formgeschichte und Verwendung im Kult des Altertums*

Diepolder, H. (1931) *Die attischen Grabreliefs des 5. und 4. Jhs. v. Chr.*

Dussler, L. (1972) *Festschrift L. Dussler*

Eco, U. and Sebeok, T. (eds.) (1983) *The Sign of Three*

Eichler, F. (1971) 'Zum Partherdenkmal von Ephesos'. *ÖJh* 49: 102–36

Elsner, J. (1995) *Art and the Roman Viewer*

(2000) 'From the Culture of Spolia to the Cult of Relics: The Arch of Constantine and the Genesis of Late Antique Forms'. *Papers of the British School at Rome* 68: 149–84

(2003) 'Style' in: Nelson and Shiff (2003): 98–109

Fehr, B. (1977) Review of T. Hölscher, *Griechische Historienbilder des 5. und 4. Jh. v. Chr.* (1973). *Gnomon* 49: 179–92

Felletti Maj, B. M. (1977) *La tradizione italica nell'arte romana*

Fink, J. (1964) 'Ein Kopf für viele'. *RM* 71: 152–7

Fittschen, K. (1982) 'Die Bildnistypen der Faustina Minor und die Fecunditas Augustae'. *AbhGöttingen* 3. Series no. 126

Fittschen, K. and Zanker, P. (1985) *Katalog der römischen Porträts in den Capitolinischen Museen und den anderen kommunalen Sammlungen der Stadt Rom* I

Flach, D. (1973) *Tacitus in der Tradition der antiken Geschichtsschreibung*

Flashar, H. (1984) 'Die Poetik des Aristoteles und die griechische Tragödie'. *Poetica* 16: 1–23

Foster, H. (ed.) (1983) *Postmodern Culture*

Franciscis, A. de (ed.) (1982) *La regione sotterrata dal Vesuvio* (*Atti del convegno internazionale 11–15 Novembre 1979*)

Fritz, K. von (1958) 'Die Bedeutung des Aristoteles für die Geschichtsschreibung' in: Fondation Hardt, *Entretiens sur l'antiquité classique* 4: *Histoire et historiens dans l'antiquité*: 83–128

Fuchs, W. (1959) *Die Vorbilder der neuattischen Reliefs*
(1963) *Der Schiffsfund von Mahdia*
Fuhrmann, H. (1931) *Philoxenos von Eretria*
Furtwängler, A. (1900) *Die antiken Gemmen*
Gabba, E. and Schiarone, A. (eds.) (1989) *Storia di Roma IV: Caracteri e morfologie*
Gärtner, H. A. (1986) 'Erzählformen bei Sallust'. *Historia* 35: 449–73
Gasparri, C. (1983–4) 'Sculture provenienti dalle Terme di Caracalla e di Diocleziano'. *RIA* ser. iii 6–7: 133–50
Gell, A. (1998) *Art and Agency: An Anthropological Theory*
Ginzburg, C. (1983) 'Morelli, Freud and Sherlock Holmes: Clues and the Scientific Method' in: Eco and Sebeok (1983): 81–118
Giuliani, L. (1977) 'Alexander in Ruvo, Eretria und Sidon'. *AntK* 20: 26–42
(1986) *Bildnis und Botschaft*
Gombrich, E. H. (1953) 'Renaissance Artistic Theory and the Development of Landscape Painting'. *Gazette des Beaux-Arts* 41: 335–60
(1968) 'Style' in: Sills (1968): 352–61
Graeve, V. von (1970) *Der Alexandersarkophag und seine Werkstatt*
Grassinger, D. (1991) *Römische Marmorkratere*
Gregory, A. P. (1994) ' "Powerful Images": Responses to Portraits and Political Uses of Images in Rome'. *JRA* 7: 80–99
Hamberg, P. G. (1945) *Studies in Roman Imperial Art*
Harrison, E. B. (1965) *Archaic and Archaistic Sculpture. The Athenian Agora*, vol. XI
Hassel, F. J. (1966) *Der Trajansbogen in Benevent*
Hausmann, U. (ed.) (1969) *Allgemeine Grundlagen der Archäologie. HdArch.*
Head, B. V. (1911) *Historia Numorum* (2nd edition)
Heintze, H. von (1962) 'Drei antike Porträtstatuen'. *AntPl* 1: 28
Hesberg, H. von (1987) 'Die Löwenkampfgruppe auf dem Kapitol und ihre Wiederholung in Augsburg. Zum Problem des "Realismus" in frühhellenistischer Zeit'. *RM* 94: 109–30
Himmelmann, N. (1975) *Drei hellenistische Bronzen in Bonn. AbhMainz* no. 2
(1980) *Über Hirten-Genre in der antiken Kunst*
(1983) *Alexandria und der Realismus in der griechischen Kunst*
Holly, M. A. (1984) *Panofsky and the Foundations of Art History*
Hölscher, T. (1967) *Victoria Romana*
(1970) 'Die Victoria von Brescia'. *AntPl* 10: 67–79
(1973) *Griechische Historienbilder des 5. und 4. Jahrhunderts v. Chr.*
(1978) 'Die Anfänge römischer Repräsentationskunst'. *RM* 85: 315–57
(1980a) 'Die Geschichtsauffassung in der römischen Repräsentationskunst'. *JdI* 95: 265–321
(1980b) 'Römische Siegesdenkmäler der späten Republik' in: *Tainia: Festschrift für R. Hampe*: 351–71

(1981) Review of B. M. Felletti Maj, *La tradizione italica nell'arte romana. Gnomon* 53: 62–74
(1982) 'Ein Weiser in Heidelberg' in: *Römisches Porträt. Wissenschaftliche Zeitschrift der Humboldt-Universität zu Berlin, gesellschafts- und sprachwissenschaftliche Reihe* 31, 2/3: 213–15
(1983) *Jahrbuch der Heidelberger Akademie der Wissenschaften für das Jahr 1982*: 29–33
(1984a) 'Beobachtungen zu römischen historischen Denkmälern II'. *AA*: 283–94
(1984b) 'Actium und Salamis'. *JdI* 99: 187–214
(1984c) *Staatsdenkmal und Publikum*
(1985a) 'Die Geschlagenen und Ausgelieferten in der Kunst des Hellenismus'. *AntK* 28: 120–36
(1985b) 'Denkmäler der Schlacht von Actium'. *Klio* 57: 81–102
(1992) 'Monumenti politici di Domiziano: Stabilità e sviluppo dell'iconografia politica romana' in: *La Storia, la letteratura e l'arte a Roma, atti del convegno (Mantova Teatro Accademico 4–5, 6–7, Ottobre, 1990)*
Homeyer, H. (1965) *Lukian. Wie man Geschichte schreiben soll*
Horn, R. (1931) *Stehende weibliche Gewandstatuen in der hellenistischen Plastik. RM* Erg-H. 2
Howald, E. (1947) *Eumousia, Festgabe E. Howald*
Imdahl, M. and Kunisch, N. (1979) *Plastik. Antike und moderne Kunst der Sammlung Dierichs in der Ruhr-Universität Bochum*
Iversen, M. (1993) *Alois Riegl: Art History and Theory*
Johansen, F. S. (1971) 'Ritratti marmorei e bronzei di Marco Vipsanio Agrippa'. *AnalRom* 6: 17–48
Jucker, H. (1950) *Vom Verhältnis der Römer zur bildenden Kunst der Griechen*
Kähler, H. (1958–60) *Rom und seine Welt*
(1965) *Der Fries vom Reiterdenkmal des Aemilius Paullus in Delphi*
(ed.) (1968) *Alberti Rubeni Dissertatio de Gemma Augustea*
Kampen, N. (1995) 'On Not Writing a History of Roman Art'. *Art Bulletin* 77: 375–8
(ed.) (1996) *Sexuality in Ancient Art*
(1997) 'Democracy and Debate'. *TAPA* 127: 381–8
Kaplan, E. A. (ed.) (1988) *Postmodernism and its Discontents*
Karp, I. and Lavine, S. D. (eds.) (1991) *Exhibiting Cultures: The Poetics and Politics of Museum Display*
Kaschnitz-Weinberg, G. (1933) 'Bemerkungen zur Struktur der Altitalischen Plastik'. *Studi Etruschi* 7: 135–95
(1937) 'Ancora "la struttura" '. *La Critica d'Arte* 2: 280–4
(1965) *Kleine Schriften zur Struktur*

Kemal, S. and Gaskell, I. (eds.) (1991) *The Language of Art History*
Kinney, D. (1995) 'Rape or Restitution of the Past: Interpreting *Spolia*' in: Scott (1995): 53–67
(1997) 'Spolia, Damnatio and Renovatio Memoriae'. *MemAmAc* 42: 117–48
Kleiner, D. E. (1978) 'The Great Friezes of the Ara Pacis Augustae. Greek Sources, Roman Derivatives, and Augustan Social Policy'. *MEFRA* 90: 753–85
Kleiner, G. (1950–1) 'Das Bildnis Alexanders des Grossen'. *JdI* 65–6: 206–30
Koch, G. and H. Sichtermann (1982) *Römische Sarkophage. HdArch*
Koeppel, G. (1983) 'Die historischen Reliefs der römischen Kaiserzeit I'. *BJb* 183: 61–144
Koloski-Ostrow, A. and Lyons, C. (eds.) (1997) *Naked Truths*
Kornhardt, H. (1936) *Exemplum*
Kraus, Th. (1959) 'Das Bildnis des Antinoos'. *Heidelberger Jahrbücher* 3: 48–67
(ed.) (1967) *Das römische Weltreich, Propyläen Kunstgeschichte*, vol. II
Kroymann, J. (1956) 'Phylarchos'. *RE Supplement* 8: 471–89
Künzl, E. (1971) *Die Kelten des Epigonos von Pergamon*
Kurtz, D. (ed.) (1985) *Beazley and Oxford*
Kyrieleis, H. (ed.) (1986) *Archaische und klassische griechische Plastik*, vol. II
Lang, B. (ed.) (1979) *The Concept of Style*
Lash, W. F. (1996) 'Iconography and Iconology' in: *The Grove Dictionary of Art* vol. XV: 89–98
Latte, K. (1958) Discussion Contribution in: Fondation Hardt, *Entretiens sur l'antiquité classique* 4: *Histoire et historiens dans l'antiquité*: 129–45
Lau, D. (1975) *Der lateinische Begriff labor*
Lausberg, H. (1960) *Handbuch der literarischen Rhetorik*
Lauter, H. (1969) *Zur Chronologie römischer Kopien nach Originalen des 5. Jh*
Leander Touati, A. M. (1987) *The Great Trajanic Frieze*
Lehmann-Hartleben, K. (1926) *Die Trajanssäule*
Lippold, G. (1923) *Kopien und Umbildungen griechischer Statuen*
(1950) *Die griechische Plastik. HdArch*
L'Orange, H. P. (1932) 'Le statue di Marte e Venere nel tempio di Marte Ultore sul Foro di Augusto'. *SymbOslo* 11: 94–9 (= *Likeness and Icon* (1973), 103–6)
Maderna, C. (1987) *Juppiter, Diomedes und Merkur als Vorbilder für römische Bildnisstatuen*
Maginnis, H. (1990) 'The Role of Perceptual Learning in Connoisseurship: Morelli, Berenson, and Beyond'. *Art History* 13: 104–17
Marcadé, J. (1969) *Au Musée de Délos*
Marchand, S. (1996) *Down from Olympus: Archaeology and Philhellenism in Germany 1750–1970*

Marchetti-Longhi, G. (1932–3) 'Il colossale acrolito rinvenuto nell'"area sacra del Largo Argentina"'. *MemPontAc* 3: 133–203
Martin, H. G. (1987) *Römische Tempelkultbilder*
Martin, J. (1974) 'Antike Rhetorik'. *HAW*, vol. II 3
Meier, Chr. (1970) *Entstehung des Begriffs 'Demokratie'*
Melville, S. and Readings, B. (eds.) (1995) *Vision and Textuality*
Merlin, A. and Poinssot, L. (1930) *Cratères et candelabres trouvés en mer près de Mahdia*
Meyer, H. (1983) *Kunst und Geschichte*
Moreno, P. (1973) *Testimonianze per la teoria artistica di Lisippo*
Moretti, G. (1948) *Ara Pacis Augustae*
Mutschler, F.-H. (1975) *Erzählstil und Propaganda in Caesars Kommentarien*
Neer, R. (1997) 'Beazley and the Language of Connoisseurship'. *Hephaistos* 15: 7–30
Nelson, R. (1996) 'Appropriation' in Nelson and Shiff (1996): 116–28
Nelson, R. and Shiff, R. (eds.) (1996) *Critical Terms for Art History*
(eds.) (2003) *Critical Terms for Art History* (2nd edn)
Nodelman, S. (1966) 'Structural Analysis in Art and Anthropology'. *Yale French Studies* 36/37: 89–103
(1993) 'How to Read a Roman Portrait' in: D'Ambra (1993): 10–26
Noelke, P. (1967) 'Zum Kopf der "Meter" Doria Pamfili'. *BJb* 167: 38–57
Nylander, C. (1982) 'Il milite ignoto: un problema nel mosaico di Alessandro' in: de Franciscis (1982) 689–95
(1983) 'The Standard of the Great King – a Problem in the Alexander Mosaic'. *OpRom* 14: 19–37
Oberleitner, W. *et al.* (1978) *Kunsthistorisches Museum Wien: Funde aus Ephesos und Samothrake*
Olin, M. (1992) *Forms of Representation in Alois Riegl's Theory of Art*
Oltramare, A. (1941) 'Idées romaines sur les arts plastiques'. *REL* 19: 82–101
Overbeck, J. (1868) *Die antiken Schriftquellen zur Geschichte der bildenden Künste bei den Griechen*
Özgan, R. (1981) 'Bemerkungen zum grossen Gallieranathem'. *AA*: 489–510
Pächt, O. (1999) *The Practice of Art History: Reflections on a Method*
Pallottino, M. (1938) 'Il grande fregio di Traiano'. *BCom* 66: 17–56
Palma, B. (1981) 'Il piccolo donario pergameno'. *Xenia* 1: 45–84
Pandermalis, D. (1971) 'Zum Programm der Statuenausstattung in der Villa dei Papiri'. *AM* 86: 173–209
Panofsky, E. (1957) *Meaning in the Visual Arts*
(1962) *Studies in Iconology*
(1991) *Perspective as Symbolic Form*
Payne, A., Kuttner, A. and Smick, R. (eds.) (2000) *Antiquity and its Interpreters*

Peter, H. (1914) *Historicorum Romanorum reliquiae* (2nd edition), vol. I
Pfanner, M. (1983) *Der Titusbogen*
Pochmarski, E. (1990) *Dionysische Gruppen*
Podro, M. (1982) *The Critical Historians of Art*
Pollitt, J. J. (1974) *The Ancient View of Greek Art*
Preisshofen, F. and Zanker, P. (1970–1) 'Reflex einer klassizistischen Kunstanschauung beim Auctor ad Herennium'. *DArch* 4/5: 100–19
Preziosi, D. (ed.) (1998) *The Art of Art History: A Critical Anthology*
Reinsberg, C. (1984) 'Das Hochzeitsopfer – eine Fiktion'. *JdI* 99: 291–317
Riegl, A. (1901) *Die Spätrömische Kunst-Industrie nach dem Funden in Österreich-Ungarn dargestellt*
(1966) *Historische Grammatick der bildenden Kunste* (ed. K. M. Swoboda and O. Pächt)
(1985) *Late Roman Art Industry*
Ritter von Härtel, W. and Wickhoff, F. (1895) *Die Wiener Genesis*
Ritter von Härtel, W. and Wickhoff, F. (1900) *Roman Art: Some of its Principles and their Application to Early Christian Painting*
Rizzo, G. E. (1932) *Prassitele*
Robert, C. (1886) *Archäologische Märchen*
(1895) *Die Marathonschlacht in der Poikile und Weiteres über Polygnot, 18. HallWPr*
Rocca, E. La (1977) 'L'Apollo "qui citharam . . . tenet" di Timarchides: un frammento del tempio di Apollo in circo'. *BollMusCom* 24: 16–33
(1985) *Amazzonomachia*
Rodenwaldt, G. (1931) 'Das Problem der Renaissancen'. *AA*: 318–38
(1935) *Über den Stilwandel in der antoninischen Kunst, AbhBerlin*, no. 3: 1–27
(1936) 'Zur Kunstgeschichte der Jahre 220 bis 270'. *JdI* 55: 82–113
(1940) 'Römische Reliefs. Vorstufen zur Spätantike'. *JdI* 55: 12–43
Rumpf, A. (1950) 'Die schönsten Statuen Winckelmanns'. *Miscellanea academica Berolinensia*, vol. II 2: 31–43
(1962) 'Zum Alexander-Mosaik'. *AM* 77: 229–41
Salis, A.von (1947) *Antike und Renaissance*
Sauerländer, W. (1983) 'From Stilus to Style: Reflections on the Fate of a Notion'. *Art History* 6: 253–70
Scarrocchia, S. (1986) *Studi su Alois Riegl*
Schäfer, J. (1968) 'Der Poseidon von Melos'. *AntPl* 8: 55–68
Schalles, H. J. (1985) *Untersuchungen zur Kulturpolitik der Pergamenischen Herrscher im 3. Jh. v. Chr.*
Schanz, M. and Hosius, C. (1927) *Geschichte der römischen Literatur*, vol. I 4. *HAW*, vol. VIII I

Schapiro, M. (1936) 'The New Viennese School'. *Art Bulletin* 18: 258–66

(1944) Review of Morey, *Early Christian Art. The Review of Religion* 8: 165–86

(1969) 'On Some Problems in the Semiotics of Visual Art: Field and Vehicle as Image Signs' in: Schapiro (1994): 1–32

(1994) *Theory and Philosophy of Art: Style, Artist and Society*

Schefold, K. (1979) *Die Antwort der griechischen Kunst auf die Siege Alexanders des Großen, SbMünchen*, no. 4

Schlosser, J. von (1935) '"Stilgeschichte" und "Sprachgeschichte" der bildenden Kunst'. *SbMünchen* 1: 3–39

(1936) '"Storia delle stile" e "storia del linguaggio" delle arti figurativi' in: *La storia dell'arte nelle esperienze e nei ricordi di un suo colore*: 175–221

Schmidt, E. (1961) *Der große Altar zu Pergamon*

(1968) 'Die Mars–Venus-Gruppe im Museo Capitolino'. *AntPl* 8: 85–94

Schmidt, G. (1970) 'Der Brunnsche Kopf'. *AntPl* 10: 29–38

Schneider, R. M. (1986) *Bunte Barbaren*

Schober, A. (1936) 'Das Gallierdenkmal Attalos' I. in Pergamon'. *RM* 51: 104–24

(1951) *Die Kunst von Pergamon*

Schrader, H. (1924) *Phidias*

Schreiber, Th. (1894) *Die hellenistischen Reliefbilder*

Schröder, S. (1986) 'Der Apollon Lykeios und die attische Ephebie des 4. Jhs.'. *AM* 101: 167–84

(1989) *Römische Bacchusbilder in der Tradition des Apollon Lykeios*

Schuchhardt, W.-H. (1977) *Alkamenes. BWPr* 126

Schwartz, E. (1897) 'Die Berichte über die catilinarische Verschwörung'. *Hermes* 32: 554–608

(1903) 'Diodoros von Agyrion'. *RE* 5, 1: 663–704

(1905) 'Duris von Samos'. *RE* 5, 2: 1854–6

Schweitzer, B. (1932) *Xenokrates von Athen*

(1969) 'Das Problem der Form in der Kunst des Altertums' in: Hausmann (1969) 163–203

Scott, S. C. (ed.) (1995) *The Art of Interpreting* (*Papers in Art History from the Pennsylvania State University* 9)

Scott Ryberg, I. (1955) 'Rites of the State Religion in Roman Art'. *MemAmAc* 22: 1–227

(1967) *Panel Reliefs of Marcus Aurelius*

Sedlmayr, H. (1959) 'Riegls Erbe'. *Hefte des Kunsthistorischen Seminars der Universität München* 4: 1–24

Settis, S. (1982) '"Ineguaglianze" e continuità: un'immagine dell'arte romana' in: Brendel (1982) 161–200

CHAPTER 2: THE GREEK PARADIGM

GREEK SCULPTURAL ANTECEDENTS

mith, *Hellenistic Ruler Portraits*, Oxford, 1988
on, *The Archaistic Style in Roman Statuary*, Leiden, 1990 (Mnemosyne
lement)
, *Greek Sculpture: An Exploration*, New Haven, 1990, esp. chapter 24
(ed.), *Not the Classical Ideal*, Leiden, 2000 (for an attempt to reverse
idealisations)

INDIVIDUAL STYLES OF GREEK SCULPTORS

and J. J. Pollitt (eds.), *Personal Styles in Greek Sculpture*, Cambridge,
(Yale Classical Studies 30)
ed.), *Polykleitos, the Doryphoros and Tradition*, Madison, Wis., 1995
elock, *The Aphrodite of Knidos and her Successors*, Ann Arbor, 1991

PORTRAITURE

ch, 'The Politics of Self-Presentation: Pliny's *Letters* and Roman
ait Sculpture' *CA* 9 (1990) 14–39
nith, 'Late Roman Philosopher Portraits from Aphrodisias' *JRS* 80
) 127–55
Hansen *et al.* (eds.), *Ancient Portraiture: Image and Message*, Copen-
, 1992 (*Acta Hyperboreana* 4)
nd A. Haeckl, 'Roman Portraiture: Reflections on the Question of
ext' *JRA* 6 (1993) 289–302
ory, '"Powerful Images": Responses to Portraits and the Political
of Images in Rome' *JRA* 7 (1994) 80–99
The Mask of Socrates, Berkeley, 1995, esp. chapter 5
nith, 'Typology and Diversity in the Portraits of Augustus' *JRA* 9
) 31–47
n, 'Seeing through Socrates: Portrait of the Philosopher in Sculpture
re' *Art History* 19 (1996) 327–52
ith, 'The Public Image of Licinius I: Portrait Sculpture and Imperial
gy in the Early Fourth Century' *JRS* 87 (1997) 170–202
, *Dynastic Commemoration and Imperial Portraiture in the Julio-*
ian Period, Cambridge, 1997
nith, 'Cultural Choice and Political Identity in Honorific Portrait
s in the Greek East in the Second Century A.D.' *JRS* 88 (1998)

ith, 'Late Antique Portraits in a Public Context: Honorific Statuary
rodisias in Caria, A.D. 300–600' *JRS* 89 (1999) 155–89

(1989) 'Un'arte plurale. L'impero romano, i Greci e i posteri' in: Gabba and Schiavone (1989): 827–78
(1999) *Laocoonte: Fama e stile*
Sgobbo, I. (1971) 'Le "danzatrici" di Ercolano'. *Rendiconti dell'Accademia di Archeologia, Lettere e Belle Arti, Napoli*, n.s. 46, 51–74
Sichtermann, H. (1974) 'de gustibus. Zur Beurteilung des römischen Klassizismus'. *Gymnasium* 81: 1–40
Sills, D. L. (ed.) (1968) *International Encyclopedia of the Social Sciences*, vol. XV
Simon, E. (1967) *Ara Pacis Augustae*
(1984) 'Apollon/Apollo' in: *LIMC* vol. II 1: 363–446
(1986) *Augustus. Kunst und Leben in Rom um die Zeitenwende*
Simon, E. and Hirmer, M. (1976) *Die griechischen Vasen*
Skinner, Q. (1985) *The Return of Grand Theory in the Human Sciences*
Strasburger, H. (1966) *Die Wesensbestimmung der Geschichte durch die antike Geschichtsschreibung. Sitzungsberichte der Wissenschaftlichen Gesellschaft der Johann-Wolfgang-Goethe-Universität Frankfurt* 5, no. 3
Studniczka, F. (1888) 'Aus Chios'. *AM* 13: 160–201
Svoronos, J. N. (1937) *Das Athener Nationalmuseum*, vol. III
Tanner, J. (2000) 'Portraits, Power and Patronage in the Late Roman Republic'. *JRS* 90: 18–50
Torelli, M. (1982) *Typology and Structure of Roman Historial Reliefs*
(1996) 'Roman Art, 43 BC–AD 69' in: Bowman *et al.* (1996): 930–58
Toynbee, J. M. C. (1934) *The Hadrianic School: A Chapter in the History of Greek Art*
Trillmich, W. (1973) 'Bemerkungen zur Erforschung der römischen Idealplastik'. *JdI* 88: 247–82
Van Eck, C., McAllister, J. and Van der Vall, R. (eds.) (1995) *The Question of Style in Philosophy and the Visual Arts*
Vergo, P. (ed.) (1989) *The New Museology*
Vermeule, C. C. (1968) *Roman Imperial Art in Greece and Asia Minor*
Vogel, L. (1968) 'Flexibility versus Formalism'. *Art Journal* 27: 271–8
Watzinger, C. (1946–7) 'Theoxenia des Dionysos'. *JdI* 61/62: 76–87
Weber, M. (1978) 'Der Kopf der Amazone Mattei'. *JdI* 93: 175–83
(1984) 'Die Amazonen von Ephesos II'. *JdI* 99: 75–126
Wegner, M. (1966) *Die Flavier. Das römische Herrscherbild*, vol. II 1
Wehrli, F. (1947) 'Die Geschichtsschreibung im Lichte der antiken Theorie' in: Howald (1947) 54–71
Wenning, R. (1978) *Die Galateranatheme Attalos I*
Willers, D. (1975) *Zu den Anfängen der archaischen Plastik in Griechenland*
Whitley, J. (1997) 'Beazley as Theorist'. *Antiquity* 71: 40–7
Wind, E. (1985) *Art and Anarchy*

Winkes, R. (1985) *Late Roman Art Industry*
Witkin, R. (1995) *Art and Social Structure*
Wojcik, M. R. (1986) *La villa dei Papiri ad Ercolano*
Wollheim, R. (1973) *On Art and Mind*
(1979) 'Pictorial Style: Two Views' in: Lang (1979): 129–45
(1980) *Art and its Objects*
(1995) 'Style in Painting' in: Van Eck *et al.* (1995): 37–49
Wölfflin (1950) *Principles of Art History*
Wood, C. (1991) 'Introduction' in: Panofsky (1991): 7–24
(ed.) (2000) *The Vienna School Reader: Politics and Art Historical Method in the 1930s*
Wünsche, R. (1972) 'Der Jüngling vom Magdalensberg. Studie zur römischen Idealplastik' in: Dussler (1972) 45–80
Zanker, P. (1973) *Studien zu den Augustus-Porträts* I: *Der Actium-Typus. AbhGöttingen* 3rd. Series, no. 85
(1974) *Klassizistische Statuen*
(1975) 'Grabreliefs römischer Freigelassener'. *JdI* 90: 267–315
(ed.) (1976) *Hellenismus in Mittelitalien. AbhGöttingen* 3rd. Series, no. 97
(1979) 'Die Villa als Vorbild des späten pompejanischen Wohngeschmacks'. *JdI* 94: 460–523
(1982) 'Herrscherbild und Zeitgeschicht'. *Römisches Porträt* (see under Hölscher (1982)): 307–12
(1983) 'Città e architettura nella Roma imperiale'. *AnalRom*, Supplement 10: 21–40
(1988) *The Power of Images in the Age of Augustus*
(1997) 'In Search of the Roman Viewer' in: Buitron Oliver (1997): 179–92
Zegers, N. (1959) *Wesen und Ursprung der tragischen Geschichtsschreibung*
Zerner, H. (1976) 'Alois Riegl: Art, Value and Historicism'. *Daedalus* 105: 177–88
(1997) 'L'art contemporain et la recuperation du passé' in: *Ecrire l'histoire de l'art*: 15–34
Ziegler, K. (1966) *Das hellenistische Epos*
Zinserling, G. (1959–60) 'Studien zu den Historiendarstellungen der römischen Republik', *Wissenschaftliche Zeitschrift der Friedrich-Schiller-Universität Jena* 9, *Gesellschafts- und sprachwissenschaftliche Reihe* 4–5: 403–48

Further rea

By JAŚ ELS

This list is primarily intended for English-
cussions of the main monuments or subj
Roman Art. In rare cases, I include non-
tance. I include only items from after 198
published.

GENER

M. Beard and J. Henderson, *Classical A* 2001
E. D'Ambra (ed.), *Roman Art in Context*,
E. D'Ambra, *Art and Identity in the Roman*
J. R. Clarke, *Art in the Lives of Ordinary R*
K. M. D. Dunbabin, *Mosaics of the Greek a*
J. Elsner, *Art and the Roman Viewer: The World to Christianity*, Cambridge, 19
J. Elsner (ed.), *Art and Text in Roman Cul*
J. Elsner, *Imperial Rome and Christian Tr AD 100–450*, Oxford, 1998
E. K. Gazda (ed.), *Roman Art in the Priva*
D. E. E. Kleiner, *Roman Sculpture*, New H
D. E. E. Kleiner and S. B. Matheson, *I, Cla* 1996
R. Ling, *Roman Painting*, Cambridge, 19
R. Ling, *Ancient Mosaics*, London, 1998
J. Onians, *Classical Art and the Cultures o*
N. H. and A. Ramage, *The Cambridge Il* bridge 1991 (2nd edition: *Roman Ar*
A. Rouveret, *Histoire et imaginaire de la Le siècle ap. J.C.*, Rome, 1989
R. Turcan, *L'Art romain dans l'histoire*, P

R. R. R.
M. Fuller sup
A. Stewa
B. Cohen som
O. Palagi 199
W. Moon
C. M. Ha
E. W. Le Port
R. R. R. S (199
J. Fischer- hage
E. Gazda Con
A. P. Gre Uses
P. Zanker,
R. R. R. S (199
J. Henders Cult
R. R. R. S Ideo
C. B. Ro *Clau*
R. R. R. S Statu 56–9
R. R. R. S in Ap

E. Bartman, *Portraits of Livia: Imaging the Imperial Woman in Augustan Rome*, Cambridge, 1999

S. Wood, *Imperial Women: A Study in Public Images, 40 BC–AD 68*, Leiden, 1999

J. Tanner, 'Portraits, Power and Patronage in the Late Roman Republic' *JRS* 90 (2000) 18–50

R. R. R. Smith, 'The Statue Monument of Oecumenius: A New Portrait of a Late Antique Governor from Aphrodisias' *JRS* 92 (2002) 134–56

HISTORICAL RELIEFS

See the bibliographically up-to-date series of articles by G. Koeppel, 'Die historischen Reliefs der römischen Kaiserzeit I–IX' *BJb* 183–92 (1983–92)

CHAPTER 3: THE MONUMENTS

ARA PACIS

S. Settis, 'Die Ara Pacis' in W. D. Heilmeyer (ed.), *Kaiser Augustus und die Verlorene Republik*, Mainz, 1988, 400–25

P. Zanker, *The Power of Images in the Age of Augustus*, Ann Arbor, 1988, 120–5, 158–61, 172–6, 179–83, 203–6

B. Kellum, 'What We See and What We Don't See: Narrative Structure in the Ara Pacis Augustae' *Art History* 17 (1994) 26–45

D. Castriota, *The Ara Pacis Augustae and the Imagery of Abundance in Later Greek and Early Roman Imperial Art*, Princeton, 1995

K. Galinsky, *Augustan Culture*, Princeton, 1996, 141–55

D. A. Conlin, *The Artists of the Ara Pacis*, Chapel Hill, 1997

CHAPTER 4: BATTLE-SCENES: HELLENISTIC

HELLENISTIC ART

Stewart (1990) chapters 17–19

R. R. R. Smith, *Hellenistic Sculpture: A Handbook*, London, 1991

M. Robertson and J. Pollitt, 'What is Hellenistic about Hellenistic Art?' in P. Green (ed.), *Hellenistic Art and Culture*, Berkeley, 1993, 67–110

A. Stewart, 'Narrative and Allusion in the Hellenistic Baroque' in P. J. Holliday (ed.), *Narrative and Event in Ancient Art*, Cambridge, 1993, 130–74

O. Pelagia and W. Coulson (eds.), *Regional Schools in Hellenistic Sculuture*, Oxford, 1998

B. S. Ridgway, *Hellenistic Sculpture* I–III, Madison, Wis., 2000–2002

ALEXANDER MOSAIC

A. Stewart, *Faces of Power: Alexander's Image and Hellenistic Politics*, Berkeley, 1993, 130–50

A. Cohen, *The Alexander Mosaic: Stories of Victory and Defeat*, Cambridge, 1997

E. Badian, 'A Note on the "Alexander Mosaic"' in T. B. Titchener and R. F. Moorton (eds.), *The Eye Expanded*, Berkeley, 1999, 75–92

CHAPTER 5: BATTLE-SCENES: ROMAN

TRIUMPH PAINTINGS

P. J. Holliday, 'Roman Triumph Painting: Its Function, Development and Reception' *Art Bulletin* 79 (1997) 130–47

P. J. Holliday, *The Origins of Roman Historical Commemoration in the Visual Arts*, Cambridge, 2002

TRAJAN'S COLUMN

S. Settis, A. La Regina, G. Agosti and V. Farinella, *La Colonna Traiana*, Turin, 1988

F. A. Lepper and S. S. Frere, *Trajan's Column: A New Edition of the Cichorius Plates*, Gloucester, 1988

P. Veyne, 'Conduct Without Belief and Works of Art Without Viewers', *Diogenes* 143 (1988) 1–22

S. Settis, 'La Colonne Trajane: L'empereur et son public' *RA* (1991) 186–98

A. Claridge, 'Hadrian's Column of Trajan' *JRA* 6 (1993) 5–22

V. Huet, 'Stories One Might Tell of Roman Art: Reading Trajan's Column and the Tiberius Cup' in Elsner (1996) 9–31

P. Davies, 'The Politics of Perpetuation: Trajan's Column and the Art of Commemoration' *AJA* 101 (1997) 41–65

M. Wilson Jones, *Principles of Roman Architecture*, New Haven, 2000, chapter 8

F. Coarelli, *The Column of Trajan*, Rome, 2000

MARCUS' COLUMN

F. Pirson, 'Style and Message on the Column of Marcus Aurelius' *PBSR* 64 (1996) 139–79

V. Huet and J. Scheid (eds.), *La Colonne Aurélienne*, Turnhout, 2000

CHAPTER 6: STATE CEREMONIAL

POLYKLEITOS AND AUGUSTAN ART

J. Pollini, 'The Augustus from Prima Porta and the Transformation of the Polykleitan Heroic Ideal: The Rhetoric of Art' in Moon (1995) 262–82

ARA PACIS AND STATE CEREMONIAL

P. J. Holliday, 'Time, History and Ritual on the Ara Pacis Augustae' *Art Bulletin* 72 (1990) 542–57

J. Elsner, 'Cult and Sculpture: Sacrifice in the Ara Pacis Augustae' *JRS* 81 (1991) 50–61

R. Billows, 'The Religious Processions of the Ara Pacis Augustae: Augustus' *supplicatio* in 13 BC' *JRA* 6 (1993) 80–92

BENEVENTUM ARCH

S. Currie, 'The Empire of Adults: The Representation of Children on Trajan's Arch at Beneventum' in Elsner (1996) 153–81

M. Torelli, '"Ex his castra, ex his tribus replebuntur": The Marble Panegyric on the Arch of Trajan at Beneventum' in D. Buitron-Oliver (ed.), *The Interpretation of Architectural Sculpture in Greece and Rome*, Washington, D.C., 1997 (Studies in the History of Art 49) 145–78.

CHAPTER 7: THE SEMANTIC SYSTEM: ELEMENTS

NEO-ATTIC STYLE

L. A. Touchette, *The Dancing Maenad Reliefs*, London, 1995

COPYING OF GREEK TYPES

E. Bartman, *Ancient Sculptural Copies in Miniature*, Leiden, 1992

M. Marvin, 'Copying in Roman Sculpture: The Replica Series' in D'Ambra (1993) 161–88

M. Marvin, 'Roman Sculptural Reproductions or Polykleitos: The Sequel' in A. Hughes and E. Ranfft (eds.), *Sculpture and its Reproductions*, London, 1997, 7–28

J. Trimble, 'Replicating the Body Politic: The Herculaneum Woman Statue Types in Early Imperial Italy' *JRA* 13 (2000) 41–68

E. Gazda (ed.), *The Ancient Art of Emulation: Studies in Artistic Originality and the Tradition from the Present to Classical Antiquity*, Ann Arbor, 2002

ANTINOÖS PORTRAITS

H. Meyer, *Antinoös: die archäologische Denkmäler unter Einbeziehung des numismatischen und epigraphischen Materials sowie der lieterarischen Nachrichten*, Munich, 1991

VILLA DEI PAPIRI

P. G. Warden, 'The Sculptural Program of the Villa of the Papyri' *JRA* 4 (1991) 257–64

P. G. Warden and D. G. Romano, 'The Course of Glory: Greek Art in a Roman Context at the Villa of the Papyri at Herculaneum' *Art History* 17 (1994) 228–54

S. Dillon, 'Subject Selection and Viewer Reception of Greek Portraits from Herculaneum and Tivoli' *JRA* 13 (2000) 21–40

HOUSE DÉCOR

E. Bartman, 'Sculptural Collecting and Display in the Private Realm' in Gazda (1991) 71–88

A. Wallace-Hadrill, *Houses and Society in Pompeii and Herculaneum*, Princeton, 1994

P. Zanker, *Pompeii: Public and Private Life*, Cambridge, Mass., 1998

S. P. Ellis, *Roman Housing*, London, 2000, 114–44

R. Tybout, 'Roman Wall-Painting and Social Significance' *JRA* 14 (2001) 33–56

S. Hales, *The Roman House and Social Identity*, Cambridge, 2003

CHAPTER 8: THE SEMANTIC SYSTEM: PREMISSES AND STRUCTURE

THEORETICAL VIEWS OF ART AND LITERARY PARALLELS

E. Leach, *The Rhetoric of Space*, Princeton, 1988

J. Onians, 'Quintilian and the Idea of Roman Art' in M. Henig (ed.), *Architecture and Architectural Sculpture in the Roman Empire*, Oxford, 1990, 1–9

J. Romm, 'Wax, Stone and Promethean Clay: Lucian as Plastic Artist' *Classical Antiquity* 9 (1990) 74–98

J. Isager, *Pliny on Art and Society*, London, 1991

J. Elsner, 'Seductions of Art: Encolpius and Eumolpus in a Neronian Picture Gallery' *Proceedings of the Cambridge Philological Society* 39 (1993) 30–47

Elsner (1995) 15–48, 51–8

J. Elsner, 'Image and Ritual: Reflections on the Graeco-Roman Appreciation of Art' *Classical Quarterly* 46 (1996) 515–31

M. Bettini, *The Portrait of the Lover*, Berkeley, 1999

J. Henderson, *Pliny's Statue: The* Letters, *Self-Portraiture and Classical Art*, Exeter, 2002

J. Small, *The Parallel Worlds of Classical Art and Text*, Cambridge, 2003

LYSIPPUS

P. Moreno (ed.), *Lisippo: L'arte e la fortuna*, Florence, 1995, esp. 290–414

PRAXITELES

A. Corso, *Prassitele: Fonti epigrafiche e letterarie. Vite e opere*, 3 vols., Rome, 1988–91

SCULPTURAL PRACTICE

P. Rockwell, *The Art of Stoneworking*, Cambridge, 1993

CHAPTER 9: THE ORIGINS OF THE SYSTEM

LATE HELLENISTIC AND EARLY ROMAN ART

E. Gruen, *Culture and National Identity in Rome*, London, 1992, 152–82
M. Torelli, *Studies in the Romanization of Italy*, Edmonton, Alberta, 1995, chapters 8–10
M. Torelli, *Tota Italia*, Oxford, 1999, chapters 3–6

Index